OPPOSING VIEWPOINTS® SERIES

Banned Books

Other Books of Related Interest

Opposing Viewpoints Series

America's Great Divide
The Future of Higher Education
The New Censorship

At Issue Series

Mob Rule or the Wisdom of the Crowd?
Public Outrage and Protest
The Role of Religion in Public Policy

Current Controversies Series

Attacks on Science
Freedom of the Press
Historical Revisionism

> “Congress shall make no law … abridging the freedom of speech, or of the press.”
>
> *First Amendment to the U.S. Constitution*

The basic foundation of our democracy is the First Amendment guarantee of freedom of expression. The Opposing Viewpoints series is dedicated to the concept of this basic freedom and the idea that it is more important to practice it than to enshrine it.

OPPOSING VIEWPOINTS® SERIES

Banned Books

Andrew Karpan, Book Editor

GREENHAVEN PUBLISHING

Published in 2024 by Greenhaven Publishing, LLC
2544 Clinton Street,
Buffalo NY 14224

First Edition

Articles in Greenhaven Publishing anthologies are often edited for length to meet page requirements. In addition, original titles of these works are changed to clearly present the main thesis and to explicitly indicate the author's opinion. Every effort is made to ensure that Greenhaven Publishing accurately reflects the original intent of the authors. Every effort has been made to trace the owners of the copyrighted material.

Cover image: Yolya Ilyasova/Shutterstock.com

Library of Congress CataloginginPublication Data

Names: Karpan, Andrew, editor.
Title: Banned books / edited by Andrew Karpan.
Description: First edition. | New York : Greenhaven Publishing, 2024. | Series: Opposing viewpoints | Includes bibliographic references and index.
Identifiers: ISBN 9781534509597 (pbk.) | ISBN 9781534509603 (library bound)
Subjects: LCSH: Prohibited books--Juvenile literature. | Challenged books--Juvenile literature. | School libraries--Censorship--Juvenile literature.
Classification: LCC Z1019.B366 2024 | DDC 098'.1--dc23

Manufactured in the United States of America

Website: http://greenhavenpublishing.com

Contents

Chapter 3: Is Book Banning Good for Education?

Chapter 4: Is Book Banning Good for Society?

The Importance of Opposing Viewpoints

Perhaps every generation experiences a period in time in which the populace seems especially polarized, starkly divided on the important issues of the day and gravitating toward the far ends of the political spectrum and away from a consensus-facilitating middle ground. The world that today's students are growing up in and that they will soon enter into as active and engaged citizens is deeply fragmented in just this way. Issues relating to terrorism, immigration, women's rights, minority rights, race relations, health care, taxation, wealth and poverty, the environment, policing, military intervention, the proper role of government—in some ways, perennial issues that are freshly and uniquely urgent and vital with each new generation—are currently roiling the world.

If we are to foster a knowledgeable, responsible, active, and engaged citizenry among today's youth, we must provide them with the intellectual, interpretive, and critical-thinking tools and experience necessary to make sense of the world around them and of the all-important debates and arguments that inform it. After all, the outcome of these debates will in large measure determine the future course, prospects, and outcomes of the world and its peoples, particularly its youth. If they are to become successful members of society and productive and informed citizens, students need to learn how to evaluate the strengths and weaknesses of someone else's arguments, how to sift fact from opinion and fallacy, and how to test the relative merits and validity of their own opinions against the known facts and the best possible available information. The landmark series Opposing Viewpoints has been providing students with just such critical-thinking skills and exposure to the debates surrounding society's most urgent contemporary issues for many years, and it continues to serve this essential role with undiminished commitment, care, and rigor.

The key to the series's success in achieving its goal of sharpening students' critical-thinking and analytic skills resides in its title—

Opposing Viewpoints. In every intriguing, compelling, and engaging volume of this series, readers are presented with the widest possible spectrum of distinct viewpoints, expert opinions, and informed argumentation and commentary, supplied by some of today's leading academics, thinkers, analysts, politicians, policy makers, economists, activists, change agents, and advocates. Every opinion and argument anthologized here is presented objectively and accorded respect. There is no editorializing in any introductory text or in the arrangement and order of the pieces. No piece is included as a "straw man," an easy ideological target for cheap point-scoring. As wide and inclusive a range of viewpoints as possible is offered, with no privileging of one particular political ideology or cultural perspective over another. It is left to each individual reader to evaluate the relative merits of each argument—as he or she sees it, and with the use of ever-growing critical-thinking skills—and grapple with his or her own assumptions, beliefs, and perspectives to determine how convincing or successful any given argument is and how the reader's own stance on the issue may be modified or altered in response to it.

This process is facilitated and supported by volume, chapter, and selection introductions that provide readers with the essential context they need to begin engaging with the spotlighted issues, with the debates surrounding them, and with their own perhaps shifting or nascent opinions on them. In addition, guided reading and discussion questions encourage readers to determine the authors' point of view and purpose, interrogate and analyze the various arguments and their rhetoric and structure, evaluate the arguments' strengths and weaknesses, test their claims against available facts and evidence, judge the validity of the reasoning, and bring into clearer, sharper focus the reader's own beliefs and conclusions and how they may differ from or align with those in the collection or those of their classmates.

Research has shown that reading comprehension skills improve dramatically when students are provided with compelling, intriguing, and relevant "discussable" texts. The subject matter of these collections could not be more compelling, intriguing, or urgently relevant to today's students and the world they are poised to inherit. The anthologized articles and the reading and discussion questions that are included with them also provide the basis for stimulating, lively, and passionate classroom debates. Students who are compelled to anticipate objections to their own argument and identify the flaws in those of an opponent read more carefully, think more critically, and steep themselves in relevant context, facts, and information more thoroughly. In short, using discussable text of the kind provided by every single volume in the Opposing Viewpoints series encourages close reading, facilitates reading comprehension, fosters research, strengthens critical thinking, and greatly enlivens and energizes classroom discussion and participation. The entire learning process is deepened, extended, and strengthened.

For all of these reasons, Opposing Viewpoints continues to be exactly the right resource at exactly the right time—when we most need to provide readers with the critical-thinking tools and skills that will not only serve them well in school but also in their careers and their daily lives as decision-making family members, community members, and citizens. This series encourages respectful engagement with and analysis of opposing viewpoints and fosters a resulting increase in the strength and rigor of one's own opinions and stances. As such, it helps make readers "future ready," and that readiness will pay rich dividends for the readers themselves, for the citizenry, for our society, and for the world at large.

Introduction

> *"Books not on the district-approved list or not approved by a certificated media specialist need to be covered or stored and paused for student use."*

—Paula Renfro, chief academic officer for Florida's Duval County School District

In October 2023, Scholastic Books decided that the popular elementary school book fairs that it regularly runs as one of the largest educational publishers in the country would now have a separate section called "Share Every Story, Celebrate Every Voice." This gesture was in response to what it calls "enacted or pending legislation in more than 30 U.S. states prohibiting certain kinds of books from being in schools—mostly LGBTQIA+ titles and books that engage with the presence of racism in our country." [1] In lieu of filing lawsuits to include its full catalog of books inside schools, the publisher had decided that the challenged books would simply be sold separately, in whatever states had not tried to ban them. According to one report, the books in this collection included "a children's biography of Supreme Court Justice Ketanji Brown Jackson; a fantasy novel about a Lakota girl; a graphic novel featuring the Black Panther superhero; and a book about different family types, such as adoptive families and families with same-sex parents." [2] Shortly after announcing this policy, Scholastic was criticized for segregating diverse titles and facilitating book banning, which caused the publisher to reverse their decision.

Any list of "banned" books is, as Katy Waldman of the *New Yorker* once put it, "a document of the culture war." [3] One of the earlier waves of book banning in the United States, assembled by Anthony Comstock (1844–1915) in the late 1800s, was notable for deciding that ideas like birth control were "obscene," reflecting what, in retrospect, were anxieties over the changing role of women in society. The most recent wave of book bans could be said to date to the early days of the Biden Administration and was fermented in pro-Trump bastions of the country like Florida. In fact, one of the most well-organized faces of the book banning efforts in schools around the country, an organization founded by a group of dissatisfied Floridian school board members called "Moms For Liberty," dates its founding to January 1, 2021, the very month Biden took office. Within two years, the state would have the second-highest number of book bans in the country, per a report from PEN America, which tallied 566 different bans in 21 school districts. [4]

Another central difference between today's book ban battles and those that took place in Anthony Comstock's days is where exactly they are happening. Seizing on the federal government's domain over what the U.S. Constitution calls "interstate commerce," limitations on content deemed to be "obscene" was handled by the U.S. Post Office, which could block and impound shipments of books between their publishers and bookstores. The idea was not limited to the United States, either; customs officers at shipping ports in various European colonial outposts would often do similarly, with their own interest in limiting the spread of foreign texts that could be seen as inciting revolution among various oppressed peoples. But a century later, the advent of the internet has largely made the idea of limiting the publication of objectionable books futile. (Though the example of China, which has instituted what Geremie Barmé has termed the "Great Firewall" in order to block access to some foreign information sources, suggests that this idea is very much not just a thing of the past in some parts of the world.) Instead, the fight in the United States has largely shifted to schools.

And it's in schools where this debate remains, animated by the voices of angry parents, the fearful concerns of school librarians, and the efforts by publishers to not let a culture war stop its lucrative sales of books, whatever they might be about. In *Opposing Viewpoints: Banned Books*, we'll look at how this debate got here and where it looks like it's going. Who knows what they will try to ban next?

Notes

[1] "A Message from Scholastic on U.S. Book Fairs," Scholastic, October 14, 2023. http://mediaroom.scholastic.com/press-release/message-scholastic-book-fairs.

[2] Dana Goldstein, "For Book Fairs, Scholastic Will Separate Titles That Deal With Race and Gender," the *New York Times,* October 16, 2023. https://www.nytimes.com/2023/10/16/us/scholastic-book-fair-diversity-censorship.html.

[3] Katy Waldman, "What Are We Protecting Children From by Banning Books?," the *New Yorker*, March 10, 2023. https://www.newyorker.com/books/page-turner/what-are-we-protecting-children-from-by-banning-books.

[4] "Banned in the USA: The Growing Movement to Censor Books in Schools," PEN America, September 19, 2022. https://pen.org/report/banned-usa-growing-movement-to-censor-books-in-schools.

OPPOSING VIEWPOINTS® SERIES

Chapter 1

Have Books Always Been Banned?

Chapter Preface

Fundamental to the debate over banning books is the idea of freedom of speech and expression. It's an idea that, in its modern form, dates to the Enlightenment, which began in the late 1600s, and the invention of the printing press, which dated to 1436 but took a while to catch on. The connection between these ideas was obvious; the spreading of new ideas primarily took place by way of the printed word, and the corresponding spread of literacy during the era gave those ideas a new audience.

At the same time, the spread of new ideas could be seen as potentially destabilizing by those in power, or who had the power to control the ways texts entered societies. Texts could represent and give voice to ideas and desires that went against popular mores or values. More dramatically, they could give voice to ideas like political revolution. Before books could be banned in schools, they could be contained at the borders.

This is why mail was at the center of many early censorship efforts, in the U.S. and elsewhere. Inspectors at customs houses would look at texts like any other potentially dangerous contaminant, parsing through thousands of words to find evidence of "offensive material," which could come in the form of languages that were considered foreign and, thus, suspicious, or what the American censorship campaigner Anthony Comstock would term "obscene."

While the freedom of expression was considered a big part of the political identity in the U.S., that didn't mean the country's polity were immune from these kinds of restraints. Comstock, in particular, would frame his campaign to limit the spread of such offensive literature around protecting "our youth," a reoccurring theme throughout the country's history of censorship. As the country became more urban and industrialized, the idea of "vice" spread easily too, a corrupting force that was often used as a scapegoat for the ways that the inequalities of a new industrial society laid waste to many a young person in those days.

Viewpoint 1

> *"Comstock's influence extended far beyond the 1873 law. In the years following the Comstock Act's passage, state lawmakers greenlit a series of related restrictions now known collectively as the Comstock laws. The scope of these measures was staggering."*

The Comstock Act and the History of Banning "Obscene" Material

Ellen Wexler

In this viewpoint, Ellen Wexler takes a look at the long history and ongoing legacy of what is known as the Comstock Act, which became law in 1873 and was named after a longtime anti-pornography crusader named Anthony Comstock. According to Wexler, Comstock had framed his concerns over "the forces of moral bankruptcy" around fears that such things would corrupt "our youth," a recurring motif among those seeking to ban certain texts from being read publicly. Wexler points out the impact the Comstock Act has had on banning literature and preventing materials related to abortion from being mailed. Ellen Wexler is a writer for Smithsonian *magazine, where this viewpoint first appeared.*

"The 150-Year-Old Comstock Act Could Transform the Abortion Debate," by Ellen Wexler, Smithsonian Magazine, June 15, 2023.

As you read, consider the following questions:

1. What did anti-vice activist Anthony Comstock mean by "our youth are in danger?"
2. What did Anthony Comstock do to help get the Comstock Act passed?
3. What is the lasting legacy of the Comstock Act?

"Our youth are in danger."

So read the urgent warning written by anti-vice activist Anthony Comstock in his 1883 book, *Traps for the Young*.

He cautioned, "Mentally and morally, they are cursed by a literature that is a disgrace to the 19th century. The spirit of evil environs them."

Each section of the text examined a new category of vice that could ensnare an unsuspecting child in evil's clutches. Chapter titles included "Free-Love Traps," "Artistic and Classical Traps," "Gambling Traps" and "Advertisement Traps."

In chapter eight, "Death-Traps by Mail," Comstock wrote of evil that is "thrust upon the youth in secret" via the postal service. Through the mail, he added, "the most infamous scoundrel may send the vilest matter to the purest boy or girl. And *this is being done systematically*."

While *Traps for the Young* is little known today, the book is steeped in the same fears that cemented Comstock's more lasting legacy ten years prior: In 1873, he successfully lobbied for the so-called Comstock Act, which criminalized sending "obscene, lewd or lascivious" materials through the mail.

The law didn't explicitly define "obscenity." But violating the measure could be punished with jail time, hard labor and fines up to $2,000. The ban covered pornographic materials, in addition to anything related to "the prevention of conception or procuring of abortion."

By the mid-20th century, the legislation was mostly meaningless, as various court rulings had stripped it of its power. But since the

Supreme Court overturned *Roe v. Wade* last June, the relevance of the Comstock Act 150 years after its passage has become an open question. As the *New York Times* reported in May, "Comstock is back, once more being wielded as a weapon by social conservatives. Their arguments use the language of the act to target the mailing of abortion pills, and they are pushing judges and the Biden administration to reopen seemingly long-settled questions."

Who Was Anthony Comstock?

Born in 1844, Comstock grew up in a large family in New Canaan, Connecticut. His father, Thomas Anthony Comstock, was a successful farmer who spent most of his time working, leaving his wife, Polly Ann Lockwood, to tend to the children. A deeply religious woman, she read to her children from the Bible and taught them to value purity. Historians later suggested that Comstock was drawn to stories like the tale of Adam and Eve, which praises the virtues of resisting temptation while warning of the dangers of succumbing to it.

When Comstock was 10, his mother died. The reverend of the family's church died around the same time. The boy was deeply affected by these losses, which strengthened his drive to carry on the ideals they lived by. As he grew older, he wrote in his diaries about his struggle to control his own sexual appetites—a struggle that "filled him with guilt and may have had much to do with his eventual calling as an anti-pornography crusader," as *Literary Hub* puts it.

In 1863, at the height of the Civil War, Comstock joined the Union Army. He was shocked by the vices he observed in his fellow soldiers. When the men received a ration of whiskey, Comstock refused to drink the spirit. Rather than surrendering his ration, he poured it out on the ground in front of the other men.

After the war, Comstock settled in New York City, finding work at a dry goods store—as well as new opportunities to rein in the vices of his colleagues. After he learned about a fellow employee who had purchased erotic literature, Comstock located the bookstore in question and turned the seller in to the police.

Comstock had found his calling. He joined forces with the Young Men's Christian Association (YMCA), which held similar views on obscenity. Backed by a like-minded community, he began efforts to forcibly suppress vice in earnest. He started small, working with police to identify sellers of illicit items.

He did not, however, destroy these materials.

Comstock called his collection of pornographic images, pulp novels and other items his "Chamber of Horrors." In 1873, he hauled the trove to Washington, D.C., where the YMCA had sent him to push for federal anti-obscenity legislation. Warning legislators of the threat posed by the forces of moral bankruptcy, he brandished the artifacts from his collection as visual aids. In Congress, he found a receptive audience. As he wrote in his diary, "All were very much excited and declared themselves ready to give me any law I might ask for, if only it was within the bounds of the Constitution."

Within weeks, Congress approved what's now known as the Comstock Act, which was signed by President Ulysses S. Grant on March 3, 1873. Lawmakers were so taken with Comstock that they went even further, appointing him as a special agent of the United States Post Office Department, an unpaid role that gave him the power to enforce his new anti-obscenity law.

Comstock "was given that title so that he could have the power to inspect the mail, and over time, it was expanded to be able to come into people's houses and seize items," Amy Sohn, author of a book about Comstock, told NPR in 2021. "It was a very broad, broad definition of what someone affiliated with the Post Office could do with regards to individual civil liberties."

Around the same time, the YMCA formed the New York Society for the Suppression of Vice, which New York state endowed with similar enforcement powers. Comstock also served as the society's secretary.

Using his newfound postal powers, Comstock made more than 50 arrests in the year following the law's implementation. He continued to work in his Post Office role for the next four decades, retiring a few months before his death in 1915. Toward the end of his life, he bragged that he had confiscated 150 tons of books, made 4,000 arrests and pushed 15 people to die by suicide.

What Did the Comstock Act Do?

Comstock's influence extended far beyond the 1873 law. In the years following the Comstock Act's passage, state lawmakers greenlit a series of related restrictions now known collectively as the Comstock laws. The scope of these measures was staggering.

"The early Comstock Act enforcement is extraordinarily broad, and gets broader and broader," Mary Ziegler, a legal scholar at the University of California, Davis, tells the *New York Times*. She adds that targeted acts could include "writing a letter to somebody asking them for a date if they weren't married."

In 1905, Irish playwright George Bernard Shaw popularized the term "Comstockery," which referred to the strict censorship of materials considered obscene. "Comstockery is the world's standing joke at the expense of the United States," wrote Shaw in the *Times* in 1905. "Europe likes to hear of such things. It confirms the deep-seated conviction of the Old World that America is a provincial place, a second-rate country-town civilization after all."

The bans' most obvious targets were erotic images and texts. But they also covered subjects that could only be considered obscene under loose definitions of the word, such as sex education texts that went to pains to circumvent the laws. In 1915, reproductive rights activist Mary Ware Dennett distributed a popular sex education booklet that omitted information about birth control. She wrote, "At present, unfortunately, it is against the law to give people information as to how to manage their sex relations so that no baby will be created." But the book was still deemed obscene, and Dennett was charged with violating the Comstock Act. (Her conviction was later overturned in a landmark free speech case.)

The Comstock laws applied to works of art and literature, too. In 1883, Comstock targeted an art gallery that sold reproductions of famous nude artworks, such as Alexandre Cabanel's *The Birth of Venus*. A court ruled against the gallery owner and seized the paintings.

Similar censorship cases continued for decades. In 1920, two women published a particularly lewd chapter of James Joyce's *Ulysses* in their literary journal. They were found guilty of distributing obscene materials through the mail and forced to shut down the publication. For the following decade, Americans interested in reading *Ulysses*—now commonly counted among the greatest novels of all time—could only do so by finding copies smuggled in from Paris.

How Did the Comstock Act Apply to Abortion and Contraception?

Under the Comstock Act, materials related to contraception or abortion were also considered obscene. As states passed additional legislation, the scope of such bans varied across the country. In Connecticut, the state with the strongest prohibitions, lawmakers banned the use of birth control outright. While the strictest bans weren't always enforced, even married couples using birth control could technically be given prison time.

In 1914, Margaret Sanger, an activist who would go on to found Planned Parenthood, started the Woman Rebel, a newsletter that provided information on birth control. Because she intended to send her materials through the mail, she was indicted for violating the Comstock Act and had to flee the country.

"When the Constitution of the United States authorized Congress to establish post offices and post roads, it was not intended that the authority should go beyond this," Sanger later wrote. "The post office was, primarily, a mechanical institution, not an ethical one, whose business was efficiency, not religion or morality."

Sanger's husband, William Sanger, stayed behind, and in 1915, he was arrested for selling a copy of "Family Limitations," an informational pamphlet about contraception written by his wife. Comstock testified against William during the ensuing trial. William was sentenced to 30 days in prison. Comstock, perhaps believing his legacy was secure, died 11 days after William's sentencing.

By the time of the moral crusader's death, public opinion was changing. The charges against Margaret Sanger were dropped a few months later. For the rest of the 20th century, the Comstock laws' power slowly declined. Some were struck down by court cases, including *Roe v. Wade*; others remained on the books but were no longer enforced. Eventually, even those that survived came to be viewed as little more than relics from the moral panics of the past.

Why Do the Comstock Laws Matter Today?

This year marked the Comstock Act's 150th anniversary. Now, following the Supreme Court's decision to strike down *Roe v. Wade* last year, the act is making headlines once again. Anti-abortion activists are citing it as they seek to criminalize the act of sending abortion pills through the mail.

Late last year, a Christian legal group called the Alliance Defending Freedom filed a lawsuit against the U.S. Food and Drug Administration (FDA). In the lawsuit, the group challenged the FDA's approval of an abortion pill called mifepristone. Originally approved in 2000, the drug ends early pregnancies by blocking the supply of certain hormones.

In April, Matthew Kacsmaryk, a Donald Trump-appointed federal judge in Texas, sided with the plaintiffs. In his ruling, which suspended the FDA's approval of the drug, he cited the Comstock Act. His opinion, as *Vox* puts it, "partially rests on the proposition that, now that *Roe* has been overruled, the Comstock Act's ban on mailing abortion medications has roared back into full effect."

From there, the case went to the U.S. Court of Appeals for the Fifth Circuit in New Orleans, which reversed the suspension of the FDA's approval. At the same time, however, it tightened the window in which mifepristone can be used from ten weeks of pregnancy to seven weeks. Crucially, it also barred delivery of the drug by mail.

Soon after, the Supreme Court temporarily blocked the new restrictions, restoring access to the drug as the case winds through the courts; a separate federal judge has now ordered the FDA to keep the drug accessible in certain states. Legal experts speculate that the matter will eventually end up at the Supreme Court, which could issue a more definitive ruling.

Depending on how the legal battle proceeds, the Comstock Act could end up having widespread consequences for those trying to access mifepristone—a group that includes patients having miscarriages. The drug is sometimes prescribed to increase the likelihood that these patients won't need to undergo a more invasive procedure.

If the law is interpreted broadly enough, the resulting restrictions could go far beyond matters of the U.S. mail. And, as legal scholars Sonia Suter and Naomi Cahn write for the *Conversation*, such an interpretation could also extend past mifepristone.

The pair argues, "While abortion remains legal in certain states, we believe it's possible that a court could interpret the Comstock Act to prevent the distribution of any tool used for an abortion, anywhere in the U.S."

Viewpoint 2

> *"As regards censorship, material was not read so much as treated like other forms of cargo, scanned for markings and sampled for traces of offensive material. Tax collectors at heart, customs officials were not keen readers."*

The Relationship Between Book Censorship and the Mail

Isabel Hofmeyr

This viewpoint looks at the historic role that custom houses had in controlling what kinds of books were allowed into the British colonies, namely by looking through some of the records tracing this practice in South Africa, which had remained a major U.K. colony until 1910. For Isabel Hofmeyr, custom houses give a window into how the language of written texts, primarily books, was being controlled by political authorities, who had their own reasons for trying to ban books containing "offensive material." According to Hofmeyr, custom officials looked at books like objects, potential carriers of political contamination; "French was suspect, non-Roman script dangerous," she writes. Hofmeyr teaches African literature at the University of the Witwatersrand and has written books like 2013's Gandhi's Printing Press: Experiments in Slow Reading.

"Colonial ports, customs and censorship: tracking books from ship to shore," by Isabel Hofmeyr, The Conversation, June 6, 2021. https://theconversation.com/colonial-ports-customs-and-censorship-tracking-books-from-ship-to-shore-161220.

As you read, consider the following questions:

1. What is "hydrocolonialism" and why did Isabel Hofmeyr invent this term?
2. How did the controls that Hofmeyr calls hydrocolonialism impact the kinds of reading material available in the British colonies?
3. Why does Hofmeyr assert that customs officials were not "keen readers?"

Some years back, I wrote a book about Mahatma Gandhi's work as a printer and publisher in South Africa, from 1893 to 1914. The man who was to become the great anti-colonial figure had arrived in Durban as a nervous young lawyer and had been rapidly drawn into defending Indian rights. Towards this end, he established a printing press and newspaper. One minor theme in the book was his steadfast opposition to copyright, which he thought hindered the free flow of ideas. Having completed the book, I wanted to investigate this thread further.

Was Gandhi's position unusual, or not? What was the situation when it came to colonial copyright?

Rather surprisingly this search led me—figuratively—to the dockside and the Custom House. As I discovered, it was the Custom House that from the mid-19th century had overseen copyright in most British settler colonies. Printed matter coming from outside these colonies had to be funnelled through port cities, where Customs officials checked to see that the material was not pirated, seditious or obscene. Customs became the part of the colonial state that oversaw both copyright and censorship.

My exploration of this system has produced another book, *Dockside Reading: Hydrocolonialism and the Custom House*, which will be out in 2022. It unfolds alongside the ocean, in the colonial port cities of late 19th and early 20th-century southern Africa, with glimpses toward other parts of the British empire.

Researching the Book

I sought out the Customs archives in South Africa with some trepidation, expecting dry and tedious reports on taxation and tariffs. Instead I found a fascinating archive teeming with objects, in some cases actual ones like swatches of fabric, labels of tinned condensed milk and packets of seeds.

The documents themselves were filled with arguments about what these items actually were: was a substance butter or margarine? Was there a difference between tea and medicinal herbs? Was a young pilchard the same as a sardine? The Custom House was far more intriguing than I had anticipated.

Had I done this project 10 or 15 years ago, I would no doubt have written a "drier" book, focusing only on the print culture implications of copyright and censorship in the Custom House without considering its location—the shore.

Though the first book, *Gandhi's Printing Press*, was in the field of Indian Ocean studies, there was not much actual sea involved. Like much scholarship on the maritime world, the ocean featured as a backdrop for human movement. But over the last decade, climate change has had a powerful impact on oceanic studies, which now grapple with the physical and biological reality of the marine world as well as its history.

Dockside Reading is an attempt to embed print culture in the field of oceanic studies, to put water and paper closer together. This move immerses print culture in the ecological setting of the port city and extends how we think about print and reading beyond the predictable contexts of the library, the class room, the home, and religious organisations.

Paper Trails from Ship to Shore

The book tracks printed matter from ship to shore and through the regulatory regimes of the southern African colonial Custom House.

It traces how dockside protocols shaped understandings of copyright and censorship. Rather than an institution associated with the rights of the author, copyright became conflated with cargo and commodity markings, especially mark of origin (such as "made in Australia"). British copyright became a token that a book had been made in Britain and was implicitly "white" and safe to admit. Colonial copyright was hence construed as a racial trademark and logistical inscription (a sign that aided the movement of an object).

As regards censorship, material was not read so much as treated like other forms of cargo, scanned for markings and sampled for traces of offensive material. Tax collectors at heart, customs officials were not keen readers. Instead, when dealing with a suspicious book, they applied the same techniques as they did to other suspect cargo: they sampled, counted, measured and touched.

John Locke and "Perfect Freedom"

John Locke (1632-1704) wrote one of the most powerful defences of individual liberty in his *Second Treatise of Government*. According to Locke, in the state of nature (i.e. before the appearance of political institutions) human beings enjoyed what he called "perfect freedom" to enjoy their persons and properties "as they think fit":

> To understand political power right, and derive it from its original, we must consider, what state all men are naturally in, and that is, a state of perfect freedom to order their actions, and dispose of their possessions and persons, as they think fit, within the bounds of the law of nature, without asking leave, or depending upon the will of any other man.
>
> A state also of equality, wherein all the power and jurisdiction is reciprocal, no one having more than another; there being nothing more evident, than that creatures of the same species and rank, promiscuously born to all the same advantages of nature, and the use of the same faculties, should also be equal one amongst another without subordination or subjection, unless the lord and master of them all should, by any manifest declaration of his will,

Rather than reading them, they inspected books as objects. Books were judged by their covers, their language or script (French was suspect, non-Roman script dangerous). Inspectors focused on outward information like title, copyright and publisher rather than content. Like other suspect cargo, objectionable books became potential carriers of contamination.

The "reading" methods of the Custom House were to feed into subsequent apartheid censorship practices in South Africa.

The literary consequences of the Custom House eddied outward from the dockside—at times onto and under the water. Customs inspectors dumped unclaimed, smuggled or banned items into the

> set one above another, and confer on him, by an evident and clear appointment, an undoubted right to dominion and sovereignty.
>
> These several passages in Locke's *Second Treatise of Government* contain in summary form the essence of the classical liberal notion of individual liberty and private property. He states in unequivocal language that human beings have "perfect freedom" to act and use their property "as they think fit"; that this right to freedom is equal for all "without subordination or subjection"; and that "all men" should be restrained from violating the rights of others and that every person has the right to defend their life and property from such invasion. By the same token, Locke also introduces a couple of ideas which are troubling to modern classical liberals, such as the idea that the law of equal liberty among men might be suspended by "the lord and master of them all" (presumably God) who has the right to "set one above another" and make him the sovereign power; that the right of self ownership of each person is limited by the fact that "one omnipotent, and infinitely wise maker" owns all mankind thus preventing one from "quit(ting) his station wilfully."
>
> **"John Locke on 'perfect freedom' in the state of nature (1689)," Liberty Fund.**

ocean, as did passengers approaching those ports where pirated reprints of copyrighted works were not permitted.

Hydrocolonialism

The term that I use to encompass these dockside protocols is "hydrocolonialism," a concept that links sea and land, empire and environment. This concept could be used to talk about a wide range of ideas. They include colonisation by way of water (maritime imperialism), colonisation of water (occupation of land with water resources, political and military control of waters), a colony on (or in) water (the ship as a miniature colony, or a penal island), colonisation through water (flooding of occupied land) and colonisation of the idea of water (as a private resource).

The concept of hydrocolonialism is useful for thinking about all forms of water in relation to colonisation and empire. It challenges the way colonisation has shaped what's considered to be important knowledge. It also looks at the knowledge created by people before they were colonised and highlights the rich pre-colonial understandings of water as a sacred resource, often inhabited by spirits, ancestors and deities.

The Custom House provides a useful vantage point from which to trace how water is colonised. We tend to think of the elements like air, water and ice as uncolonisable, because they cannot be settled or occupied. But these elements are colonised as resources to be extracted, or as dumping grounds for waste.

The long-term effectiveness of these strategies is apparent today if we turn to the ocean. From its sea bed to its surface it has been prospected, militarised, mined and claimed.

In southern Africa, coastal waters around port cities were colonised, most obviously through the extension of land into the sea through reclamation and submarine infrastructure. Another strategy of claiming the ocean was to extend land-based methods of governance over the ocean: claiming sovereignty, regulating the intertidal zone, declaring quarantine stations over areas around ships.

The practice of dumping goods in the ocean served to define the ocean as a rubbish dump, a space to be colonised by human waste. We might describe the Custom House as a "hydrocracy," ruling by and from the water's edge rather than from the desk of bureaucracy.

Dockside Reading demonstrates one site in which hydrocolonialism can be used to illuminate cultural and literary histories. The term, and others like it, is being explored in different areas. Examples include a special issue of the journal *English Language Notes* on "Hydro-criticism" and work by graduate students on the Oceanic Humanities for the Global South project, which explores pre-colonial and creolized ideas of water, and how black intellectual traditions engage with the ocean.

Viewpoint 3

> *"For centuries, intellectual and political authority came from religion and other traditional beliefs."*

The Enlightenment and Intellectual Freedom

Council on Foreign Relations

This viewpoint sketches out some of the intellectual and political background behind a movement that would eventually be called "the Enlightenment." Continuing the overall metaphor, this wave of ideas would move thinking in Europe further out of the "dark ages" and bring with it some of the fundamental values that would underpin the idea of intellectual freedom that would later be cited by proponents of free speech. Fittingly, the movement of these ideas was text-based, spreading through the publication and transportation of books. The Council on Foreign Relations is a think tank based in Washington, DC, that publishes the magazine Foreign Affairs.

As you read, consider the following questions:

1. What events does this viewpoint say set the stage for the Enlightenment?
2. How does this viewpoint say that thinking coming out of the scientific revolution contributed to the Enlightenment?

"What Is the Enlightenment and How Did It Transform Politics?," The Council on Foreign Relations, February 17, 2023. https://world101.cfr.org/historical-context/prelude-global-era/what-enlightenment-and-how-did-it-transform-politics.

3. Why does this viewpoint draw a comparison between ending the persecution of people on charges of witchcraft and the rise of Enlightenment ideas?

In 1627, officials in Cologne, Germany, accused Katharina Henot—a local postmaster and influential socialite—of witchcraft. They claimed she wielded magic, worked with the devil, and had infested a local nunnery with a plague of caterpillars. For these alleged crimes, she was repeatedly tortured and publicly executed.

While extraordinary by today's standards, Henot's case was alarmingly common for the time. Between 1520 and 1700, Europe executed tens of thousands of people—mostly women—on charges of witchcraft.

How did this happen? Surely anyone using science and reason could have deduced that such charges were ludicrous, right?

Then again, science and reason have not always prevailed.

For centuries, intellectual and political authority came from religion and other traditional beliefs. To understand the world—including phenomena such as plagues of caterpillars—people would turn to supernatural belief in witches or religious belief in Satan. And to explain political systems—like why a particular family had absolute rule over a kingdom—leaders turned to religion, claiming a divine right from God.

But during this time, a series of religious, political, and scientific upheavals began challenging the status quo, culminating in the Enlightenment—an intellectual movement in the seventeenth and eighteenth centuries that sought to improve society through fact-based reason and inquiry. The Enlightenment brought secular thought to Europe and reshaped the ways people understood issues such as liberty, equality, and individual rights. Today those ideas serve as the cornerstone of the world's strongest democracies.

This lesson explores the history of the Enlightenment and the radical ways in which Enlightenment ideas changed society for centuries to come.

What Events Set the Stage for the Enlightenment?

Prior to the Enlightenment, the Catholic Church reigned supreme as Europe's preeminent religious and intellectual leader. But during the 1500s and 1600s, several events began to challenge its hold on power.

Let's explore three of the most important developments:

Religious Reformation

In the year 1517, a German monk and professor of theology named Martin Luther pinned a list of ninety-five arguments, or theses, to the doors of a cathedral. Those theses accused the Catholic Church of corruption and abuse of power. Luther claimed that every individual possessed a connection with God and that the Church did not monopolize the path to salvation.

Luther's action produced a split within the Catholic Church and encouraged individuals to challenge the institution's previously unquestionable authority. Thanks to rising literacy rates and the invention of the printing press just decades prior, Luther's message reached a wide audience. The Bible was now being printed in the vernacular, and people began reading it for themselves rather than having priests explain it to them.

Political Upheaval

Europe reached a state of near-constant conflict in the 1500s, as leaders fought over land, resources, and competing interpretations of Christianity. An entire century of religious wars culminated in one of history's deadliest conflicts: The Thirty Years' War (1618–48).

Two major consequences emerged from that conflict. First, the resulting peace helped establish the bedrock principle of international relations known as sovereignty—the concept that guarantees countries get to control what happens within their borders and prohibits meddling in another country's domestic affairs. Second, it produced further criticism of the continent's political and religious leaders after decades of combat had claimed millions of lives.

Scientific Revolution

In the early 1600s, English philosopher Francis Bacon revolutionized intellectual thought by demonstrating that scientific discovery could not be achieved through faith and religion but rather rigorous research and observation. His scientific method set the gold standard for future research. It also coincided with a wave of breakthroughs in the fields of astronomy, mathematics, and physics by scientists such as Galileo Galilei, Johannes Kepler, and Isaac Newton.

Although many of those intellectuals were devout Christians who believed that science and religion were easily reconcilable, religious authorities nonetheless viewed those discoveries as threats to their power. Officials, for instance, placed Galileo under house arrest for his writings on how the earth revolved around the sun, which undermined the teachings of the Catholic Church.

Despite protestations from the Church, this era—known as the Scientific Revolution—led to a flourishing of empirical thought in Europe.

How Did the Enlightenment Transform Society?

On the heels of the Scientific Revolution came the Enlightenment—a movement that sought to apply similar methods of inquiry and discovery to the fields of law, religion, economics, and politics. Enlightenment scholars believed that such thinking could produce societies that were more equitable, just, and not beholden to the unchecked power of monarchs and religious leaders.

Let's explore five influential ideas that emerged from the Enlightenment in the seventeenth and eighteenth centuries:

Opposition to Absolute Monarchy

Intellectuals such as Jean-Jacques Rousseau and John Locke introduced the idea that no ruler should have unlimited power. Both argued that leaders derived their authority not from God but from the people. And Locke claimed that if the people opposed their leader, they had the right to replace their government with one that respected their rights.

Notably, few Enlightenment thinkers called for democracy as people understand the term today. Many intellectuals such as Voltaire believed that monarchy was the best way to advance social, political, and economic goals. However, the idea that citizens could hold their leaders accountable was revolutionary.

Separation of Powers

The Baron de Montesquieu argued that power should not be concentrated in just one person. Instead, he called for a balanced distribution of power between executive, legislative, and judicial authorities.

Enlightenment thinkers similarly called for a separation of church and state—the idea that government should not interfere in religious affairs, and vice versa. Writers such as Voltaire were highly critical of religion's outsize influence in European policymaking, which had contributed to generations of conflict on the continent.

Liberty and Individual Rights

John Locke introduced the idea that all men possess natural rights to life, liberty, and property. Those rights, he argued, were inalienable, meaning they could not be taken away or constrained by law.

Calls for individual rights contributed to increased religious tolerance in Europe as various governments began providing religious minorities greater freedom to worship.

Equality

Pre-Enlightenment Europe was highly unequal, with powerful individuals known as the nobility possessing exclusive rights to own land, avoid taxes, and hold privileged jobs, while the poorest members of society struggled to survive. The Enlightenment challenged this arrangement, as thinkers like Locke argued that all men were created equal and that no one should be born into more power than another.

However, many intellectuals believed that such equality only applied to white men. Rousseau saw groups such as women, ethnic minorities, and enslaved people as inherently inferior to white men. Nevertheless, marginalized groups often used those same Enlightenment arguments to advance their own cases for equality. English thinkers such as Mary Astell and Mary Wollstonecraft wrote extensively in support of women's access to the same rights and opportunities as men.

Free-Market Capitalism

Scottish economist Adam Smith railed against the era's prevailing economic policies such as mercantilism, in which each country sought to produce as much as possible domestically and import as little as possible from abroad. Through careful observation and research, Smith came to introduce groundbreaking economic theories—including supply and demand, free-market capitalism, comparative advantage, and minimal regulations—arguing that countries become richer when they make what they are best at producing and import what they are not. Those ideas continue to form the backbone of international trade.

Where Did the Enlightenment Inspire Revolution?

As Enlightenment texts spread across the Atlantic, their ideas inspired revolutions.

Political and intellectual leaders in Britain's thirteen American colonies used Enlightenment values to justify their declaration of independence in 1776. Following the American Revolution, those Enlightenment principles—including liberty, equality, and individual rights—became enshrined in the U.S. Constitution, even though many rights were initially reserved mostly for landowning white men. It would take nearly a century for the United States to abolish the institution of slavery and several decades longer to extend the right to vote to women.

News of the United States' Enlightenment-inspired revolution ricocheted around the world. In 1788, Thomas Jefferson—then the

U.S. minister to France—wrote to George Washington, noting that France "has been awaked by our revolution, they feel their strength, they are enlightened, their lights are spreading, and they will not retrograde." Indeed, the following year France experienced its own revolution, which ultimately toppled the country's monarchy.

In 1791, the inhabitants of France's most profitable colony—Haiti, then known as Saint-Domingue—began demanding their own right to liberty and equality. Enslaved Haitians outnumbered slaveholders ten to one on the island. After a thirteen-year war, the Haitians defeated the French and established the first Black-led republic. European powers, however, did not immediately recognize Haiti as an independent country and instead forced Haiti to pay reparations to France over more than a hundred years.

In the early 1800s, Enlightenment-educated leaders such as Simón Bolívar led movements for independence in Bolivia, Colombia, Ecuador, Peru, and Venezuela. However, while revolutionaries pledged to eliminate the colonial era's racial and social hierarchies, independence rarely brought about equality. Instead, leaders frequently perpetuated the same unequal, undemocratic systems that benefited the landowning elite.

Across Latin America—as in the United States, France, and Haiti—Enlightenment values began the march toward fairer and more equitable societies, but it would take generations for many countries to begin fully realizing those ideals.

Where Do We See Enlightenment Values Today?

More than three centuries after John Locke wrote about the relationship between people and their government, the core tenets of his writing and those of his Enlightenment contemporaries continue to shape society. Many of the world's strongest democracies, for example, actively support liberty, equality, and individual rights through their laws and norms.

But just as leaders did not universally accept Enlightenment ideas in Locke's time, the same holds true today.

Many societies—above all, authoritarian countries—actively reject some or most of the Enlightenment's founding principles. Governments in countries such as China, Egypt, Iran, North Korea, Russia, and Saudi Arabia quash civil liberties, oppose free and fair elections, reject perceived checks to their power, and—in certain instances—ignore separation of church and state.

Enlightenment ideas have even come under attack in democratic countries such as Brazil, Hungary, the Philippines, and Turkey. Leaders there have attempted to increase their power by undermining political freedoms and civil liberties in a trend known as democratic backsliding. As a result, the world has become less free and less democratic every year between 2005 and 2019.

The United States, as well, has long struggled to embrace all tenets of the Enlightenment. Inequality and systemic racism remain significant challenges, and sharp disparities persist in access to housing, wealth, education, and health care. Further, many in the United States dismiss facts and scientific inquiry; former President Donald J. Trump, for example, repeatedly sidelined top scientific experts while endorsing unproven COVID-19 medical treatments. And on January 6, 2021, the country's free and fair elections came under direct assault when armed rioters—many with white supremacist ties—stormed the U.S. Capitol seeking to overturn the results of the presidential race.

Although trials for witchcraft are no longer a normal part of life around the world, many countries still have a long way to go before fully embodying the founding principles of the Enlightenment.

Viewpoint 4

"However, freedom of speech and expression is not always absolute."

Free Speech and Its Limits

Signature Theatre

This viewpoint gives an explanation of where the U.S. Constitution has generally landed on ideas like free speech, which are often cited in fights over issues like book bans. Namely, these are outlined by looking at their outer limits, the kinds of speech that have historically been hard to protect in the courts. In the modern world, most battles of books often end up in the courts. Before appearing here, this viewpoint first appeared on the website of the Signature Theatre, an off-Broadway nonprofit theatre in New York City.

As you read, consider the following questions:

1. What are some of the common limitations to the freedom of speech?
2. Why do you think that political speech carries the highest level of political protection?
3. What are some of the security threats that are used as reasons to limit speech?

"Whoever would overthrow the liberty of a nation must begin by subduing the freeness of speech."

– *Benjamin Franklin*

The First Amendment is clear that Congress cannot make any laws that limit the freedom of the press. The First Amendment's primary goal for the press is to prevent the government from censoring it. Under these circumstances, censorship often means preventing the press from publishing information in the first place, though this can also mean punishing news organizations after they have published a story. Censorship of the press before a story is published in print, broadcast on television, radio or the internet is called "prior restraint," and the Supreme Court ruled that it was unconstitutional in a case called *Near v. Minnesota* (1931).

In this case, *The Saturday Press* was published a story stating that the city of Minneapolis, including the mayor and the chief of police, was under the secret control of a group of Jewish gangsters. City officials obtained an order to shut down the publication of the newspaper entirely and gave the editors the opportunity to go before a local judge to prove the story was true. The judge upheld the city officials' injunction stopping the publication of *The Saturday Press* and said that if the publishers continued, they would be found in contempt of court. Instead of shutting down production, the newspaper counter-sued, claiming that Minneapolis and Minnesota were violating their freedom of the press. The case made it to the Supreme Court, and they agreed that no government was allowed to censor the press because a free press is essential for the political system to work. They based their decision on historical events and statements including the following statement from British legal authority, William Blackstone:

> *The liberty of the press is indeed essential to the nature of a free state; but this consists in laying no previous restraints upon publications and not in freedom from censure from criminal matter when published.*

Citizens need a free press for many reasons, including the ability to to criticize the government or expose any of its potential wrongdoings. Left unchecked by the press, the government could potentially commit all sorts of things its citizens would disapprove of.

That being said, some issues pose such important security threats that the government is allowed to block the press from publishing about them. Military plans and movements are an example—enemy combatants could gain an advantage by reading about plans in a news source, so the government does have the right to prevent newspapers from printing that kind of information.

Posting information after events have happened is typically legal but there are some instances where that may prove problematic for publishers and editors. In *The New York Times v. United States*, the primary concern centered on whether the *Times* could publish the *Pentagon Papers*. These were secret documents outlining the history of the U.S.'s involvement in Vietnam in the 1940s, 50s, and 60s, and they showed that the federal government had lied about the scope and purpose of the war. Defense Department employee Daniel Ellsberg stole a copy of the papers and gave them to *The New York Times*, who debated about whether to publish. The government tried to stop *The New York Times* as well as *The Washington Post* from writing about the *Pentagon Papers*, since publishing would have hurt the government's image and possibly turned public opinion of the war, which was already quite sour. The court ruled in favor of the *Times*, further strengthening the First Amendment's defense of the free press.

Freedom of Speech

Freedom of speech is a principle that supports the freedom of an individual or a community to voice their opinions and ideas without fear of retaliation, censorship or sanction by the government. The term "freedom of expression" often includes any act of seeking, receiving and imparting information or ideas, regardless of the medium used.

However, freedom of speech and expression is not always absolute. Common limitations to freedom of speech relate to slander, obscenity, pornography, sedition, incitement, fighting words, classified information, copyright violation, trade secrets, food labeling, non-disclosure agreements, the right to privacy, the right to be forgotten, public security, and perjury.

Freedom of speech allows for public criticism of the government. The First Amendment protects you from the government attempting to suppress your speech. The U.S. Founders pushed for this freedom to be included in the Constitution.

While some types of speech are protected by the First Amendment, not all levels of speech have the same protection:

Political Speech

This has the highest level of protection. Political speech occupies a place in the legal system of America that is called "preferred position." This means that any law or regulation or presidential act that limits political speech is almost always struck down by the courts. The main court case that solidified this preferred position was *Brandenburg v. Ohio* in 1968. In this case, a KKK member was making a speech that as you can imagine was offensive to a lot of people and could have been considered threatening as well. The court ruled that because the speech was political, it was protected by the First Amendment no matter how outrageous it was.

Symbolic Speech

Also protected by the First Amendment. Symbolic speech includes wearing armbands, carrying signs, or wearing things with words that are directed at a military draft, police, etc. This also includes burning the flag, which is pretty much always a political message. Not all symbolic speech is protected though. These include references to obscenity, fighting words, child pornography, blackmail and threats.

Hate Speech

This form of speech is protected even if it is really hateful. This includes burning a cross on someone's lawn, although that may be prosecuted as vandalism or trespassing.

Commercial Speech

Speech that proposes a commercial transaction (ads on TV, online, radio, newspapers, etc.) are not typically protected by the First Amendment, but political commercials by campaigns and advocacy groups are. Spending money on political campaigns has been determined to be speech that is protected by the First Amendment.

Reminder! The First Amendment just protects you from government action, not the actions of private people or businesses. For example, if you work for a private company, your boss can definitely fire you for saying mean things about them or revealing company secrets. You don't have a First Amendment claim against them. However, if your boss is the government you probably do have the opportunity to issue a First Amendment case.

A specific example: in *Pickering v. Board of Education* (1942) a public-school teacher wrote a letter to the editor of the local paper complaining about the school board's usage of funds. He didn't write the letter on school time or on school paper. The school board fired him. He brought the case to the Supreme Court, claiming he was fired for a speech that was political in nature, criticizing local government and not for anything related to his job performance. And he won. Unless your employer is the government, you often cannot claim First Amendment rights for being fired.

Viewpoint 5

> *"The First Amendment serves not only the needs of the polity, but also those of the human spirit—a spirit that demands self-expression.... to suppress expression is to reject the basic human desire for recognition and affront the individual's worth and dignity."*

Legal Arguments for Free Expression

David Hudson

In this viewpoint, David Hudson looks at how court cases over the past century have clarified the social benefits of free expression. For its believers, like Hudson and former Supreme Court Justice Benjamin Cardozo, free speech is "the indispensable condition" that underpins all other freedoms and rights that define a free society. For Hudson, the freedom to speak and publish are one and the same as the freedom to think about what one wishes, a point of view that has proven popular in the courts; it's there where some of the most significant findings on the subject have been made law. David Hudson is a law professor at Belmont University and is the author, co-author, or co-editor of more than 40 books, according to the Foundation for Individual Rights and Expression, where he's also a prominent voice.

As you read, consider the following questions:

1. What are some of the reasons that the free speech theorists and scholars that Hudson cites say freedom of speech is important?
2. Why does the author of this viewpoint think that using the marketplace metaphor for free speech rights is helpful but incomplete?
3. What does Hudson mean when he says that free expression is a kind of "safety valve?"

The matrix, the indispensable condition, of nearly every other freedom"— that's how Justice Benjamin Cardozo referred to freedom of speech.

This eminent Justice is far from alone in his assessment of the lofty perch that free speech holds in the United States of America. Others have called it our blueprint for personal liberty and the cornerstone of a free society. Without freedom of speech, individuals could not criticize government officials, test their theories against those of others, counter negative expression with a different viewpoint, or express their individuality and autonomy.

The First Amendment of the United States Constitution provides that "Congress shall make no law . . . abridging the freedom of speech." This freedom represents the essence of personal freedom and individual liberty. It remains vitally important, because freedom of speech is inextricably intertwined with freedom of thought.

"First Amendment freedoms are most in danger when the government seeks to control thought or to justify its laws for that impermissible end," warned Justice Anthony Kennedy in *Ashcroft v. Free Speech Coalition* (2002). "The right to think is the beginning of freedom, and speech must be protected from the government because speech is the beginning of thought."

There are numerous reasons why the First Amendment has a preferred position in our pantheon of constitutional values. Here are six.

Self-Governance and a Check Against Governmental Abuse

Free speech theorists and scholars have advanced a number of reasons why freedom of speech is important. Philosopher Alexander Meiklejohn famously offered that freedom of speech is essential for individuals to freely engage in debate so that they can make informed choices about self-government. Justice Louis Brandeis expressed this sentiment in his concurring opinion in *Whitney v. California* (1927): "[F]reedom to think as you will and to speak as you think are means indispensable to the discovery and spread of political truth."

In other words, freedom of speech is important for the proper functioning of a constitutional democracy. Meiklejohn advocated these ideas in his seminal 1948 work, "Free Speech and Its Relation to Self-Government." Closely related to this is the idea that freedom of speech serves as a check against abuse by government officials. Professor Vincent Blasi referred to this as "the checking value" of free speech.

Liberty and Self-Fulfillment

The self-governance rationale is only one of many reasons why freedom of speech is considered so important. Another reason is that freedom of speech is key to individual fulfillment. Some refer to this as the "liberty theory" of the First Amendment.

Free-speech theorist C. Edwin Baker writes that "speech or other self-expressive conduct is protected not as a means to achieve a collective good but because of its value to the individual." Justice Thurgood Marshall eloquently advanced the individual fulfillment theory of freedom of speech in his concurring opinion in the prisoner rights case *Procunier v. Martinez* (1974) when he wrote: "The First

Amendment serves not only the needs of the polity, but also those of the human spirit—a spirit that demands self-expression. Such expression is an integral part of the development of ideas and a sense of identity. To suppress expression is to reject the basic human desire for recognition and affront the individual's worth and dignity."

The Search for Truth and the 'Marketplace of Ideas' Marketplace

Still another reason for elevating freedom of speech to a prominent place in our constitutional values is that it ensures a search for truth.

Justice Oliver Wendell Holmes expressed this idea in his "Great Dissent" in *Abrams v. United States* (1919) when he wrote that "the ultimate good desired is better reached by free trade of ideas—that the best test of truth is the power of the thought to get itself accepted in the competition of the market." This language from Holmes led to one of the most pervasive metaphors in First Amendment jurisprudence—that of the "marketplace of ideas."

This concept did not originate with Holmes, as John Milton in the 17th century and John Stuart Mill in the 19th century advanced the idea that speech is essential in the search for truth in their respective works, "Areopagitica" (1644) and "On Liberty" (1859). Milton famously wrote: "Let [Truth] and Falsehood grapple, whoever knew Truth put to the worse, in a free and open encounter?" For his part, Mill warned of the "peculiar evil of silencing the expression of an opinion" explaining that "[i]f the opinion is right, they are deprived of the opportunity of exchanging error for truth; if wrong, they lose what is almost as great a benefit, the clearer perception and livelier impression of truth, produced by its collision with error."

Informational Theory

The marketplace metaphor is helpful but incomplete. Critics point out that over the course of history, truth may not always prevail over false ideas. For example, Mill warned that truth sometimes doesn't triumph over "persecution." Furthermore, more powerful individuals may have greater access to the marketplace and devalue the contributions of others. Another critique comes from those who advocate the informational theory of free speech.

"If finding objective truth were the only value of freedom of expression, there would be little value to studying history," explains Greg Lukianoff of FIRE. "*Most* of human thought in history has been mistaken about its assumptions and beliefs about the world and each other; nevertheless, understanding things like superstitions, folk medicine, and apocryphal family histories has significance and value."

Under this theory, there is great value in learning and appreciating what people believe and how they process information. Lukianoff calls the metaphor for the informational theory of free speech "the lab in the looking glass." The ultimate goal is "to know as much about us and our world as we can," because it is vitally "important to know what people really believe, especially when the belief is perplexing or troubling."

Safety Valve Theory

Another reason why freedom of speech is important relates to what has been termed the "safety valve" theory. This perspective advances the idea that it is good to allow individuals to express themselves fully and blow off steam.

If individuals are deprived of the ability to express themselves, they may undertake violent means as a way to draw attention to their causes or protests. Justice Brandeis advanced the safety valve theory of free speech in his concurring opinion in *Whitney v. California* (1927) when he wrote:

> Those who won our independence believed . . . that it is hazardous to discourage thought, hope and imagination; that fear breeds repression; that repression breeds hate; that hate menaces stable government; that the path of safety lies in the opportunity to discuss freely supposed grievances and proposed remedies.

Tolerance Theory

Free speech has also been construed to promote the virtue of tolerance: If we tolerate a wide range of speech and ideas, this will promote greater acceptance, self-restraint, and a diversity of ideas.

Lee Bollinger advanced this theory in his 1986 work "The Tolerant Society." This theory helps explain why we should tolerate even extremist speech. As Justice Holmes wrote in his dissent in *United States v. Schwimmer* (1929), freedom of speech means "freedom for the thought that we hate." This means that we often must tolerate extremist speech. As Chief Justice John G. Roberts, Jr. wrote in *Snyder v. Phelps* (2011), we don't punish the extremist speaker; instead "we have chosen a different course—to protect even hurtful speech on public issues to ensure that we do not stifle public debate."

Conclusion

Freedom of speech holds a special place in American law and society for many good reasons.

As Rodney Smolla writes in "Free Speech in an Open Society," "[t]here is no logical reason . . . why the preferred position of freedom of speech might not be buttressed by multiple rationales." Freedom of speech is closely connected to freedom of thought, an essential tool for democratic self-governance; it leads to a search for truth; it helps people express their individuality; and it promotes a tolerant society open to different viewpoints.

In sum, it captures the essence of a free and open society.

Viewpoint 6

> *"The attacks on books in the 1980s bear similarities to the current attacks. Both object to the critical teaching about race and racism, historical as well as contemporary. Both accuse schools of tearing down America and weakening patriotism."*

Today's Book Bans Resemble Book Banning Debates from the 1980s

Fred L. Pincus

In this viewpoint, Fred L. Pincus discusses the relationship between today's book bans and attacks on books from the 1980s. In particular, Pincus points out that both of these attacks on books focus on similar issues, especially discussions of race and racism. The book-banning attempts of the 1980s were often led by Reverend Jerry Falwell and other conservative Christians, who argued that certain types of literature would weaken social institutions, morality, and patriotism. In this sense, Pincus argues that the book bans from the 1980s and today are somewhat different, in that the 1980s bans focused on fighting secular humanism, while the main target of today's book bans is critical race theory. However, despite these differences, understanding the debates from the 1980s sheds light on today's book bans. Fred L. Pincus is an emeritus professor of sociology at the University of Maryland, Baltimore County.

As you read, consider the following questions:

1. According to Pincus, why was secular humanism the "bogeyman" in 1980s book-banning efforts?
2. What erroneous allegations does Pincus say right-wing critics have made about critical race theory?
3. According to data cited in this viewpoint, how many educational gag order bills had been introduced between January 2021 and March 2022?

A conservative leader found fault with how "respect for our nation's heritage" had been mostly stripped from the textbooks of public schools.

"From kindergarten right through the total school system, it almost seems as if classroom textbooks are designed to negate what philosophies previously had been taught," the conservative leader lamented. "[M]any textbooks are actually perverting the minds of literally millions of students."

A teachers organization shot back, saying the underlying motive for some attacks against books has "unquestionably been racial."

This might sound like a back-and-forth from recent debates over removing books from school classrooms and libraries. Often, critical race theory—an academic framework for understanding racism—has been at the center of these debates. But in reality, both quotes are more than 40 years old.

Religious Influence on Politics

The first quote came from a 1981 book by the Rev. Jerry Falwell titled "Listen, America!" Falwell, founder of the Moral Majority, was one of the leaders of the book-banning efforts of the 1980s. It was during this period—with Ronald Reagan in the White House—that Christian fundamentalists became a growing influence in conservative American politics.

The second quote comes from a 1981 publication of the National Council of Teachers of English, "The Students' Right to

Read." The council was one of the major groups opposing Falwell and other conservatives.

The attacks on books in the 1980s bear similarities to the current attacks. Both object to the critical teaching about race and racism, historical as well as contemporary. Both accuse schools of tearing down America and weakening patriotism. Both object to teaching about gender roles, sexual orientation and alternative models of the family. Conservative institutions like the Heritage Foundation have been involved in both periods.

There are also important differences between the two periods. The 1980s bogeyman was secular humanism, because it argued that human beings can define their own morality without the use of religion. Falwell and others claimed that public schools were anti-Christian because they taught students that they didn't have to use the Bible as a standard for right and wrong. Chaos would result, the Christian fundamentalists asserted, if everyone had to determine their own morality.

In a way reminiscent of the so-called Scopes Monkey Trial in 1925, conservatives objected to the teaching of evolution as a fact, rather than a theory. Instead, they wanted biology textbooks to give equal space to the so-called scientific theory of creationism, which holds that God created the universe.

A New Bogeyman

In 2022, of course, the bogeyman is critical race theory. Emerging from critical legal theory taught in law schools, critical race theory argues that white supremacy has been embedded in American legal and educational institutions since the time of slavery.

Right-wing critics have made a number of erroneous allegations about critical race theory: that it is taught in public schools; that it is Marxist; that it is intended to make whites feel guilty; and more. The Heritage Foundation has published "How to Identify Critical Race Theory" as a guide to help parents evaluate books and curricula by looking for words like "systemic racism," "white privilege" and "social construction or race."

In fact, these concepts predated critical race theory, which came on the scene in the late 1970s and 1980s. Activist Stokely Carmichael—also known as Kwame Ture—and political scientist Charles V. Hamilton discussed institutional racism in "Black Power: The Politics of Liberation in America" in 1967. "Institutional racism" and "structural racism" are very similar to "systemic racism."

"White privilege" was discussed by W.E.B. Du Bois in the early 20th century and by civil rights activists in the 1950s and 1960s. Another term associated with critical race theory, "the social construction of race," was used by anthropologists like Franz Boas back in the 1950s.

New Interpretations

Critical race theorists took these and other concepts, reinterpreted them and applied them to the American legal system. Scholars in education have done the same in trying to understand education as an institution. After 40-plus years of teaching and writing about race and diversity, I know that it is impossible to accurately discuss American racial conflict without using these concepts. But that's what many lawmakers would have American educators do.

According to a Pen America report, a nonprofit that advocates for freedom of expression in literature, 156 "educational gag order" bills in 39 states have been introduced since January 2021. Twelve have become law in 10 states, and 113 are pending in 35 states. As of March 2022, at least seven states specifically ban the teaching of critical race theory. "Cumulatively," says the Pen report, "they represent a national assault on our education system, censoring both what teachers can say and what students may learn."

Of course, some white students—and other students, too, for that matter—will feel uncomfortable upon learning not only about the history of American racism but also its present manifestations. Reality is sometimes uncomfortable.

That's where good teaching comes in. Good teaching means taking the students' age into account. It also means being supportive of students who may feel uncomfortable or guilty about certain events in American history.

I always tell students: "You are not responsible for what happened in the past. You are responsible to decide what you plan to do in the present and the future."

Periodical and Internet Sources Bibliography

The following articles have been selected to supplement the diverse views presented in this chapter.

"Bannings and Burnings in History," Freedom to Read Foundation, 2019. www.freedomtoread.ca/resources/bannings-and-burnings-in-history.

Joseph M. Adelman, "Mobilizing the Public Against Censorship, 1765 and 2012," the *Atlantic*, January 23, 2012. www.theatlantic.com/technology/archive/2012/01/mobilizing-the-public-against-censorship-1765-and-2012/251830.

Teresa M. Bejan, "The Two Clashing Meanings of 'Free Speech,'" the *Atlantic,* December 2, 2017. www.theatlantic.com/politics/archive/2017/12/two-concepts-of-freedom-of-speech/546791.

Amy Brady, "The History (and Present) of Banning Books in America," LitHub, September 22, 2016. https://lithub.com/the-history-and-present-of-banning-books-in-america/.

Eshana Dasanjh, "The Censorship of the History of the British Empire," the *GSAL Journal,* January 9, 2020. thegsaljournal.com/2020/01/09/the-censorship-of-the-history-of-the-british-empire.

Chris Klimek, "A Brief History of Banned Books in America," *Smithsonian*, October 5, 2023. www.smithsonianmag.com/history/a-brief-history-of-banned-books-in-america-180983011/.

Jacob Mchangama and Jonathan Rauch, "What We Can Learn from the History of Free Speech," Cato Institute, May/June 2022. www.cato.org/policy-report/may/june-2022/what-we-can-learn-history-free-speech.

Michael Ng, "When Silence Speaks: Press Censorship and Rule of Law in British Hong Kong, 1850s–1940s," *Law & Literature*, July 4, 2017. www.tandfonline.com/doi/abs/10.1080/1535685X.2017.1327695.

Eileen Reynolds, "We the Protestors: How America's Founders Forged the Freedom of (Ugly, Vitriolic) Speech," New York University, June 30, 2016. www.nyu.edu/about/news-publications/news/2016/june/stephen-solomon-on-revolutionary-dissent.html.

Charlotte Lydia Riley, “When the British Empire Waged War on Free Speech,” the *Tribune*, April 20, 2021. tribunemag.co.uk/2021/04/pernicious-messaging.

Matthew Taub, “America’s First Banned Book Really Ticked Off the Plymouth Puritans,” *Atlas Obscura*, November 1, 2019. www.atlasobscura.com/articles/americas-first-banned-book.

Matthew White, “The Enlightenment,” the British Library, June 21, 2018. www.bl.uk/restoration-18th-century-literature/articles/the-enlightenment.

OPPOSING VIEWPOINTS® SERIES

Chapter 2

Is Book Banning Legal and Justifiable?

Chapter Preface

These days, book bans are often a matter for the courts to decide. But this hasn't made arguments about them any clearer, legally speaking. When the Supreme Court was tasked with trying to answer the question of whether schools could remove books that school board members found objectionable in the 1982 case *Board of Education, Island Trees Union Free School District v. Pico*, the justices were unable to come up with a single answer and, instead, issued at least six.

At the center of many of these book banning fights is a tension between the principles of democratic rule and its realities. Book bans in schools often come from a place of popular resentment that finds its expression in the politics of school boards, which are implicitly hard to regulate nationally. After all, the idea goes, why shouldn't a local community be able to control what books are being taught in their schools?

Opponents, however, disagree. Often times, those who wish to censor materials in classrooms are not the same people who are supposed to use the books to teach their lessons plans. Critics say that the wave of interest in book bans that had been sparked by some of the latest culture wars in the early 2020s could have the impact of shutting a generation off from some of the essential literature their parents might have read with ease at their age.

When Steve Pico went to court to fight a book ban in his junior year of high school, he observed that the titles being pulled from the shelves weren't even coming from local parents, but from a pamphlet some of the school board members had gotten their hands on and had then spread around. In a way, the current fight is little different. The current culture war frequently targets books that aim to represent LBGTQIA+ life and racial issues in literature, which has given a different character and energy to the current debate. Book ban opponents, for instance, say this means that book bans could be considered a form of discrimination.

Viewpoint 1

"While some plays were approved without a license, dramas containing blasphemous or obscene language and scenes of a sexual nature had the offending passages removed. Others were denied a license altogether."

Censorship Laws and the Theater

Kate Dossett

In this viewpoint, Kate Dossett examines the "archive of surveillance" established by the British government between 1737 and 1968 in order to monitor and censor works that were getting performed on stage in the UK. According to Dossett, censors would cut out blasphemous or obscene language as well as overtly sexual scenes. But doing this under the legal imprimatur of the state also created an immense archive of all the things that were censored or not censored, allowing patterns to be uncovered in the types of material that was censored. For instance, Dossett notes that many of the works included in the archive from the mid-20th century were created by Black playwrights. Kate Dossett is a professor of American History at the University of Leeds.

As you read, consider the following questions:

1. Why did the British government collect, monitor, and frequently censor new dramas?
2. What are some of the benefits that the writer sees in having an archive of surveillance?
3. Do you think this writer thinks censorship of those plays was a good idea?

In an age of so-called "cancel culture" it's important to remember that for much of British history it was the state, not the masses, who censored the work of artists.

Between 1737 and 1968 British theatre censorship laws required theatre managers to submit new plays intended for the professional stage to the Lord Chamberlain's Office for examination and licensing. This was necessary under the Stage Licensing Act of 1737 and the Theatres Act of 1843.

In essence, this meant that the government collected, monitored and frequently censored new dramas. In this way, the licensing of plays has inadvertently produced an extensive historical archive of surveillance and censorship. This includes records of early Black theatre-making, at a time when the British state did not routinely collect and preserve the work of Black playwrights.

The Lord Chamberlain Play's Collection, held at the British Library, contains theatre manuscripts as well as play readers reports and correspondence between theatre managers and the Lord Chamberlain's officers which document the decision-making of the censor. While some plays were approved without a license, dramas containing blasphemous or obscene language and scenes of a sexual nature had the offending passages removed. Others were denied a license altogether.

The collection includes a number of plays by Black theatre makers that were well known in their time but have since fallen into obscurity. These include *At What a Price*, written in 1932 by Una Marson, the BBC broadcaster, poet, playwright and anti-racist activist who moved from Jamaica to London in the 1930s. The play explores women's desires for love and for a career, as well as interracial relations, sexual harassment in the workplace and women's friendships.

The archive also holds a copy of *Appearances*, a courtroom drama written in 1925 by African American entrepreneur Garland Anderson who set up a milkbar in London's theatre district. The Broadway (1944) and West End (1947) hit, *Anna Lucasta*, was in the archive, too. The censors objected to the use of U.S. swear words which had to be removed before *Anna Lucasta* could be licensed.

The play explores the possibilities of redemption for the "fallen woman," Anna, a sex worker whose family renounce her only to lure her home in the hope of marrying her off to an honest young man with a bit of money.

It was originally written by a white American author and was rewritten by the American Negro Theatre with an all-Black cast. It ran for a year in the West End between 1947 and 1948.

The Archive Comes to Life

As part of a project looking at archives of surveillance, I worked with a group of theatre makers, researchers and archivists to examine the plays. We wanted to find out what issues were important to Black theatre-makers and how they navigated white gatekeepers, including the censors and theatre managers who controlled the British theatre industry in the early 20th-century.

Researchers and curators were able to identify and contextualise the plays, while theatre-makers considered what it would be like to stage these plays today. Would we reinstate lines censored by the Lord Chamberlain? Were there parts of the play directors might want to cut? And what to do with the censor's reports—particularly those which contained racially offensive language?

Inspired by what we discovered, we created a performance of staged readings directed by Dermot Daly and Eleanor Manners. We used the manuscripts and censors' reports on two plays by Black theatre-makers first staged in the West End nearly a century ago to bring them to life for a modern audience. We chose Una Marson's *At What a Price* (1933) and *In Dahomey* (1903), one of the first musical comedies written almost entirely by Black theatre-makers and presented by Black performers in the U.S. and Britain.

Separated by 30 years, and hailing from different parts of the African diaspora, these plays capture the diversity and excitement of Black performance culture in Britain in the early decades of the 20th-century. But while our project opened up access to these theatre manuscripts, it clearly does not make up for the years of invisibility.

The Power of Encounter

In her recent biography of the Black playwright Lorraine Hansberry, Soyica Colbert, a professor of African American studies and performing arts, explains the importance of "encounter" for Hansberry both as a playwright and as a political activist.

Hansberry understood encounter as not simply an interaction between two individuals but a process in need of an audience: "A knowing or understanding look from a spectator," she says, "disrupts the totalising effect of another's gaze," and resists "racism's power to isolate individuals."

It is well understood that witnesses—or an audience—are central to theatrical work. But to witness and affirm is important to encounters with the archive too. Indeed, watching, hearing, reading and performing these manuscripts together opened up new ways of using censorship archives.

These plays by Black theatre-makers as well as the censor's reports are now free to view on the British Library's Digital Manuscripts platform. It cannot right the state's wrongdoing but reclaiming these neglected texts and creating opportunities for new encounters with them constitutes a form of redress.

Viewpoint 2

> *"A violation of free speech and academic freedom, this effort is also a deeply dangerous assault on fundamental principles of teaching and learning."*

Banning Books Violates the Right to Free Speech and Harms Students

David Wippman and Glenn Altschuler

This viewpoint makes the case that banning books hurts students most. By limiting the kinds of resources teachers can use to teach, education will suffer, David Wippman and Glenn Altschuler assert. This argument reflects the territory claimed in a notable 2020s culture war that took place during the early Biden administration. It also demonstrates anxieties over changing narratives surrounding American history, which became an issue of concern in the years after the popularity of the Black Lives Matter movement. David Wippman is president of Hamilton College in Clinton, New York, and Glenn Altschuler teaches American studies at Cornell University.

As you read, consider the following questions:

1. What does this viewpoint say is at the heart of the current effort to ban books?

"OPINION: When books are banned, 'education is impoverished, and everyone loses,'" by David Wippman and Glenn Altschuler, The Hechinger Report, September 28, 2021.

2. In what way does limiting what books people read in schools limit their education?
3. Do you think teachers are better equipped than outside activists in determining how to teach students?

A year ago, a Pennsylvania school board voted to ban a long list of books and other materials relating to race and social justice. Among the banned books were children's stories about Rosa Parks and Martin Luther King, Jr., the autobiography of Nobel laureate and youth activist Malala Yousafzai and CNN's "Sesame Street" town hall on racism.

The ban was recently reversed in response to widespread criticism, but it is emblematic of an ongoing campaign by state and local officials around the country to dictate how K-12 and college and university educators and students address race, history and social justice.

Legislators in at least 27 states have proposed or enacted bans on teaching critical race theory and other so-called divisive concepts, with significant penalties attached. In Texas, a school board recently suspended and then voted not to renew the contract of a popular high school principal, apparently because he declared in a letter to the community that systemic racism is "alive and well."

A violation of free speech and academic freedom, this effort is also a deeply dangerous assault on fundamental principles of teaching and learning.

Book banning in America has a long and inglorious history, going back to the 1600s, when books deemed offensive to Christianity were publicly burned. "Uncle Tom's Cabin," the most popular novel of the 19th century, was banned throughout the Confederacy for its anti-slavery themes. In 1873, Congress passed the Comstock Act, which prohibited sending "obscene, lewd, or lascivious" materials through the mail, a definition deemed broad enough to include anatomy textbooks, "anything by Oscar Wilde, and even 'The Canterbury Tales.'"

James Joyce's "Ulysses" was banned in the 1920s, and a host of great works of literature have subsequently been banned. Such bans are eventually seen as ill advised, even absurd, but considerable harm can be done, especially in schools, while they're in place.

As we have argued elsewhere, at the heart of the current efforts is deep-seated disagreement "over whether and to what extent racism is embedded in American history and institutions, how racism should be acknowledged and combatted, and who bears responsibility for ongoing racial discrimination and injustice."

Many conservative legislators, school board members and parents object to all claims that racism in America is systemic, arguing instead that it is the product of individual bias. In opposition to anti-racist programs adopted in the wake of George Floyd's murder and the social justice reckoning it prompted, conservatives have urged instead, in then-President Donald Trump's words, a "patriotic education."

How a Teen Took on Book Banning in Schools

Book banning is a simple but sinister form of censorship that hinders a student's education rather than improving it. As a high school student in 1976, Steven Pico recognized the hazards of censorship and led the challenge to book banning in his school district. Earlier this week, the National Coalition Against Censorship's (NCAC's) Debra Lau Whelan interviewed Pico in honor of the 31st anniversary of *Board of Education, Island Trees Union Free School District v. Pico* (1982), the first school library book-banning case to be decided by the Supreme Court. What began as one student's quest to put library books back on the shelves became a historic court case in which the Court reaffirmed the principles underlying *Tinker v. Des Moines Independent Community School District* (1969), which held that students do not" shed their constitutional rights to freedom

In their view, teaching American history as a story of "oppression and victimhood" misrepresents the past and divides the country along racial lines. Texas' legislation on teaching social studies, adopted in June, reflects this conservative critique. It prohibits teaching that slavery and racism are "anything other than deviations from, betrayals of, or failures to live up to, the authentic founding principles of the United States, which include liberty and equality."

The United States has been, in many ways, a beacon of democracy and freedom. But presenting the past or the present only and always in a favorable light does an enormous disservice to students, teachers and the truth.

How can history teachers present the three-fifths clause of the U.S. Constitution, slavery, the Civil War, de jure and de facto segregation or racial disparities in housing and education without considering issues of systemic racism?

of speech or expression at the schoolhouse gate." Although FIRE [Foundation for Individual Rights and Expression] focuses solely on civil rights in higher education, Pico's comments on junior and high school censorship are important to remember regardless of the context: For me, censorship was not simply a right-wing vs. left-wing issue, and I tried my best to frame the debate on censorship my own way. I believe censorship is offensive to the vast majority of Americans, offensive to Americans from the right, offensive to Americans from the center, and offensive to Americans from the left. FIRE's Will Creeley recently emphasized precisely this point in the context of protecting speech on college campuses. Pico ends on an optimistic note; he believes" more young people are informed and passionate about their rights, and responsibilities to stand up despite the cost, today than at any previous time in American history." Indeed, a quick look at FIRE's work reveals the inspiring number of students willing to do what it takes to protect their rights on campus.

"Steven Pico, Supreme Court Victor, on Book Banning in Schools," by Sarah McLaughlin, Foundation for Individual Rights and Expression, July 11, 2013.

How can English teachers discuss Ralph Ellison's "Invisible Man," Philip Roth's "The Human Stain" or Toni Morrison's "Beloved" without considering race and social justice? Should discussions of the Civil Rights bills of 1964 and 1965, George Wallace and current debates about voter suppression be banished from political science and civics classes?

Good teaching demands subject matter expertise, the ability to distinguish facts from interpretations—while analyzing the relationship between them—and a willingness to present a wide range of views on controversial subjects.

Teachers should be able to exercise their professional judgment on how best to present challenging material, without fearing that open discussion will endanger their jobs or lead to civil or criminal penalties.

And students will learn best how to think critically; construct, critique and defend arguments; and develop their intellectual, social and moral faculties when they grapple with difficult subjects in age-appropriate ways.

When school boards or legislators with little or no subject matter or pedagogical expertise ban books or direct how certain subjects should be taught, education is impoverished, and everyone loses. This principle applies without regard to the political basis for censorship. While, at the moment, pressures are coming principally from the right, educators also face pressures from the left. Among the ten most frequently challenged books of 2020 were Harper Lee's "To Kill a Mockingbird" and John Steinbeck's "Of Mice and Men," both deemed offensive for their inclusion of racial slurs and racist stereotypes.

It's understandable that politicians and parents want to weigh in, but decisions about what to teach and how to teach it should be left to the professionals.

Viewpoint 3

> *"Whether any of these efforts are unconstitutional censorship is a complex question."*

The Legality and Constitutionality of Book Banning Is Complicated

Erica Goldberg

In this viewpoint, Erica Goldberg asserts that debates over how schools regulate what books are in their libraries are a little more complicated than most would expect. Additionally, these regulations might also not be against the law. For instance, control over public education is considered to be a provenance of "state and local authorities," according to the Supreme Court, which often means those officials have control over setting curricula in schools. But this doesn't mean they can impose extreme bans on content. The courts have also ruled, for instance, that one state-level law that banned teachers from covering the topic of evolution was unconstitutional, because it suggested the state was endorsing an official religious answer to that cosmic question. Erica Goldberg is an associate professor of law at the University of Dayton.

"When are book bans unconstitutional? A First Amendment scholar explains," by Erica Goldberg, The Conversation, April 13, 2022. https://theconversation.com/when-are-book-bans-unconstitutional-a-first-amendment-scholar-explains-176225.

As you read, consider the following questions:

1. What types of books are generally banned by those on the political Right? What types are banned by the political Left?
2. Why does Goldberg think that the question of whether censorship efforts in schools are unconstitutional is a complex one?
3. What are the First Amendment rights that students do have?

The United States has become a nation divided over important issues in K-12 education, including which books students should be able to read in public school.

Efforts to ban books from school curricula, remove books from libraries and keep lists of books that some find inappropriate for students are increasing as Americans become more polarized in their views.

These types of actions are being called "book banning." They are also often labeled "censorship."

But the concept of censorship, as well as legal protections against it, are often highly misunderstood.

Book Banning by the Political Right and Left

On the right side of the political spectrum, where much of the book banning is happening, bans are taking the form of school boards' removing books from class curricula.

Politicians have also proposed legislation banning books that are what some legislators and parents consider too mature for school-age readers, such as "All Boys Aren't Blue," which explores queer themes and topics of consent. Nobel Prize-winning author Toni Morrison's classic "The Bluest Eye," which includes themes of rape and incest, is also a frequent target.

In some cases, politicians have proposed criminal prosecutions of librarians in public schools and libraries for keeping such books in circulation.

Most books targeted for banning in 2021, says the American Library Association, "were by or about Black or LGBTQIA+ persons." State legislators have also targeted books that they believe make students feel guilt or anguish based on their race or imply that students of any race or gender are inherently bigoted.

There are also some attempts on the political left to engage in book banning as well as removal from school curricula of books that marginalize minorities or use racially insensitive language, like the popular "To Kill a Mockingbird."

Defining Censorship

Whether any of these efforts are unconstitutional censorship is a complex question.

The First Amendment protects individuals against the government's "abridging the freedom of speech." However, government actions that some may deem censorship—especially as related to schools—are not always neatly classified as constitutional or unconstitutional, because "censorship" is a colloquial term, not a legal term.

Some principles can illuminate whether and when book banning is unconstitutional.

Censorship does not violate the Constitution unless the government does it.

For example, if the government tries to forbid certain types of protests solely based on the viewpoint of the protesters, that is an unconstitutional restriction on speech. The government cannot create laws or allow lawsuits that keep you from having particular books on your bookshelf, unless the substance of those books fits into a narrowly defined unprotected category of speech such as obscenity or libel. And even these unprotected categories are defined in precise ways that are still very protective of speech.

The government, however, may enact reasonable regulations that restrict the "time, place or manner" of your speech, but generally it has to do so in ways that are content- and viewpoint-neutral. The government thus cannot restrict an individual's ability to produce or listen to speech based on the topic of the speech or the ultimate opinions expressed.

And if the government does try to restrict speech in these ways, it likely constitutes unconstitutional censorship.

What's Not Unconstitutional

In contrast, when private individuals, companies and organizations create policies or engage in activities that suppress people's ability to speak, these private actions don't violate the Constitution.

The Constitution's general theory of liberty considers freedom in the context of government restraint or prohibition. Only the government has a monopoly on the use of force that compels citizens to act in one way or another. In contrast, if private companies or organizations chill speech, other private companies can experiment with different policies that allow people more choices to speak or act freely.

Still, private action can have a major impact on a person's ability to speak freely and the production and dissemination of ideas. For example, book burning or the actions of private universities in punishing faculty for sharing unpopular ideas thwarts free discussion and unfettered creation of ideas and knowledge.

When Schools Can 'Ban' Books

It's hard to definitively say whether the current incidents of book banning in schools are constitutional—or not. The reason: Decisions made in public schools are analyzed by the courts differently than censorship in nongovernment contexts.

Control over public education, in the words of the Supreme Court, is for the most part given to "state and local authorities." The government has the power to determine what is appropriate for students and thus the curriculum at their school.

However, students retain some First Amendment rights: Public schools may not censor students' speech, either on or off campus, unless it is causing a "substantial disruption."

But officials may exercise control over the curriculum of a school without trampling on students' or K-12 educators' free speech rights.

There are exceptions to government's power over school curriculum: The Supreme Court ruled, for example, that a state law banning a teacher from covering the topic of evolution was unconstitutional because it violated the establishment clause of the First Amendment, which prohibits the state from endorsing a particular religion.

School boards and state legislators generally have the final say over what curriculum schools teach. Unless states' policies violate some other provision of the Constitution—perhaps the protection against certain kinds of discrimination—they are generally constitutionally permissible.

Schools, with finite resources, also have discretion to determine which books to add to their libraries. However, several members of the Supreme Court have written that removal is constitutionally permitted only if it is done based on the educational appropriateness of the book, but not because it was intended to deny students access to books with which school officials disagree.

Book banning is not a new problem in this country—nor is vigorous public criticism of such moves. And even though the government has discretion to control what's taught in school, the First Amendment ensures the right of free speech to those who want to protest what's happening in schools.

Viewpoint 4

> *"In the weeks following that meeting, more than 125 books were pulled from Granbury ISD school library shelves. About 75 percent of those could be described as LGBTQ-themed."*

New Legal Questions About Banning Books

Kelley R. Taylor

This viewpoint by Kelley R. Taylor takes the position that the law is somewhat unclear on the issue of banning books. The last time the issue came before the Supreme Court, the resulting ruling was splintered between six different justices and "left no clear precedent," according to Taylor. It's likely, Taylor writes, that a somewhat newer high court could take up the issue. This is because some of the legal challenges that have been leveled by groups like the American Civil Liberties Union, among others, stake ground on ideas like the possibility of using civil rights laws to challenge school-wide book bans. Kelley R. Taylor has been a features writer at School Library Journal, *a teachers trade magazine, since 2018.*

As you read, consider the following questions:

1. What's the connection between book banning in the contemporary culture war and documented anti-LGBTQ sentiment?

"Are Book Bans a Civil Rights Violation? A Federal Investigation into a Texas District Will Decide," by Kelley R. Taylor, School Library Journal, January 28, 2023.

2. The viewpoint talks about an "age-old dilemma tied to book banning." What is this dilemma?
3. How clear does Taylor think the law is about banning books?

Attempts to ban books continue in school board meetings across the country, but increasingly, the conversation has moved to statehouse legislators and lawyers. More than 10 states have introduced legislation that would make it easier to remove titles from school library shelves. Librarians and their fellow educators fear legal prosecution. And students, who identify personally with the themes and topics in many of the banned books, report feeling disenfranchised and discriminated against.

That's the case in Texas, where a book ban challenge brought by the ACLU has led to a federal investigation. Opened in December, that investigation will consider whether book bans, which are often argued to be an infringement of First Amendment rights, are also a violation of civil rights. The ACLU of Texas says yes. But will the federal government agree and provide a new legal avenue for fighting to keep books on library shelves?

In January 2022, the superintendent of Granbury ISD, Jeremy K Glenn, had a meeting with librarians in which he reportedly instructed them to remove books with LGBTQ themes from library shelves. The meeting was recorded, and investigative coverage from NBC News, ProPublica, and *The Texas Tribune* revealed Glenn's comments.

"There are two genders," Glenn is reportedly heard saying on the recording. "There's male, and there's female. And I acknowledge that there are men that think they're women. And there are women that think they're men. And again, I don't have any issues with what people want to believe, but there's no place for it in our libraries."

According to reporting, Glenn described Granbury as being in a very conservative community with very conservative members on the school board, as well as saying of the content of the titles that needed to be removed, that it's the "transgender, LGBTQ, and the sex—sexuality—in books."

In the weeks following that meeting, more than 125 books were pulled from Granbury ISD school library shelves. About 75 percent of those could be described as LGBTQ-themed, according to the ACLU of Texas. In July 2022, the organization filed a complaint with the U.S. Department of Education, saying the Granbury action violates Title IX of the Education Amendments of 1972.

"Superintendent Glenn's comments and the resultant purge of LGBTQ+ books from library shelves by district employees plainly were discriminatory acts and create a pervasively hostile atmosphere for LGBTQ+ students in Granbury ISD," the Texas ACLU said in its complaint.

In response, in December, the Department of Education's Office for Civil Rights opened an investigation into the Granbury ISD book ban. While that sounds significant, opening a federal investigation into a civil rights complaint is not uncommon. However, this investigation's focus—whether the Granbury book ban is a form of discrimination based on gender identity and sexual orientation—is somewhat novel. Will this approach and federal investigation have a significant impact on other censorship attempts across the country?

Just Another Book Removal?

The Granbury ISD book removal is another in a proliferation of book bans in the last few years. In Texas alone, about 800 books were banned in a 12-month period from 2021 to 2022, according to PEN America. Additionally, data from the American Library Association indicates that more than 1,600 books were targeted for removal from libraries across the country in 2022.

Legal action challenging various book bans has been initiated and is ongoing in other places as well.

Last year, in Missouri, the Wentzville R-IV district was sued for removing eight titles that included memoirs and novels addressing race, gender, and sexual identity. In challenging the Wentzville book ban, the ACLU of Missouri focused on censorship and equal protection.

"School boards cannot ban books because the books and their characters illustrate viewpoints different of those of the school board; especially when they target books presenting the viewpoints of racial and sexual minorities, as they have done in Wentzville," the ACLU argued.

Essentially, the Missouri ACLU said that Wentzville district failed to use established and unbiased procedures for book removal and that the banned books were "removed on an arbitrary basis and not in a viewpoint neutral manner."

Since that lawsuit was filed, the Wentzville board has put several of the challenged books back on school library shelves but has permanently banned other titles. The case is an example of a typical pattern that book bans and legal challenges to those bans have followed over the years.

A key difference with the Granbury ISD complaint is that the ACLU of Texas is saying that documented anti-LGBTQ sentiment was the reason the books at issue were removed from district libraries. And because of that, the removal amounts to illegal discrimination against LGBTQ students. Specifically, the ACLU of Texas argues that Glenn and Granbury ISD violated Title IX—and that argument, in the book ban context, is a new approach.

Title IX was originally designed to prevent discrimination based on sex in education programs and activities. But over time and especially after the U.S. Supreme Court upheld the right of LGBTQ employees to be free from workplace discrimination in 2020, the breadth of Title IX's application has grown. In June of 2021, President Biden and the U.S. Department of Education adopted the interpretation that Title IX's prohibition on the "basis of sex" includes discrimination based on sexual orientation and gender identity.

Not all states have embraced that application of the civil rights law. Attorneys general from 12 states challenged the Department's interpretation. In July 2022, the Department of Education was preliminarily enjoined from implementing its interpretation of Title IX in those states.

Texas, however, is not one of those states. So, the ACLU's assertion that the Granbury book ban violates Title IX relies on the Department of Education's interpretation of the civil rights law. One aspect surrounding the book ban that seems to bolster the ACLU's claim is the well-documented statements of the Granbury ISD superintendent. There are also other facts and circumstances that the ACLU says point to anti-LGBTQ sentiment as the rationale for the book removal.

For example, Granbury ISD's communications director reportedly acknowledged that some people would not agree with the book ban. But in justifying the book removal, the director added, "We understand the conservative climate of our community and that a large majority recognizes that several social and cultural topics are best left to parents and families to discuss with their children."

Who Should Decide?

The Granbury communication director's statement underscores an age-old dilemma tied to book banning, which is the question of who (i.e., parents, school boards, courts, or state legislatures) should decide what books kids have access to in school libraries.

For decades, that question has spurred usual legal arguments when book bans come about. One is that banning books in public school libraries is a form of censorship (e.g., a violation of the First Amendment to the U.S. Constitution) or of equal protection. Others contend that book removals are merely a matter of proper school authority and that school districts have broad discretion to decide what materials do, or do not, belong on school library shelves. That notion is long-established. But the law surrounding how much discretion schools have when they remove books from school library shelves is less clear.

The last time the U.S. Supreme Court decided a book banning case (*Pico vs. Island Trees School District*) was more than 40 years ago, producing a ruling with six differing opinions from the nine justices. It left no clear precedent, therefore there is no definitive way to say if a district's removal of books amounts to a violation of the U.S. Constitution or of civil rights laws or a simple legal exercise of local district oversight.

The federal investigation into Granbury ISD's book ban will take time—maybe a long time. And it's way too early to speculate whether the complaint will eventually reach the Supreme Court or what would happen if it got there. Meanwhile, librarians in Granbury and across the country remain on the frontlines of the battle for intellectual freedom and, perhaps, in defense of students' civil rights.

> *"I believe censorship is offensive to the vast majority of Americans, offensive to Americans from the right, offensive to Americans from the center, and offensive to Americans from the left."*

Teens Played an Important Role in Legally Preventing Book Banning

Debra Lau Whelan

In this viewpoint, Steven Pico speaks with Debra Whelan about his involvement in a historical case in front of the Supreme Court, Board of Education, Island Trees Union Free School District v. Pico, *which was the first—and so far, only—time that the high court made its opinions known on the issue of banning books. While Pico was still in high school, he found out about a book removal program that had been initiated when members of the board that ran his school "found" a list of "objectionable" books on a table at a conference and decided to purge the school library of those books, which included notable modern classics like* Slaughterhouse-Five *and* Go Ask Alice. *Debra Lau Whelan is a development director at National Coalition Against Censorship.*

"NCAC Talks to the Man Behind *Pico v. Board of Ed*," by Debra Lau Whelan, National Coalition Against Censorship, July 9, 2013.

As you read, consider the following questions:

1. Why does Steven Pico say that concern with censorship is offensive to Americans on both sides of the aisle?
2. How long was Pico's life consumed by the Supreme Court case?
3. Does Pico think book bans are ever justified?

Steven Pico may not be a household name. But for those who champion the freedom to read, he's a big deal. Back in 1976, Pico and four other teens sued their school district in Long Island, NY, for banning 11 books from their classrooms and school libraries.

The six-year battle to defend the constitutional rights of these students made history. The case landed in the Supreme Court, and the *Board of Education, Island Trees Union Free School District v. Pico* became the first school library book-banning case to ever reach the high court.

Pico has spent more than 30 years as an editor, and he's also a painter and sculptor who exhibits his works in France, Portugal, and the U.S. We caught up with him on the 31st anniversary of the landmark June 25, 1982, decision to talk about why he did it, the impact it's had on his life, and whether he thinks kids today are as passionate about free speech as he was.

It's been over 30 years since the Supreme Court ruling. Are you surprised that so many books are still being challenged and banned in schools and libraries nationwide?

Changes in constitutional law take place gradually. If one looks at any major issue affecting life in the U.S., from the transformation of colonies into 50 states or to racial equality, for example, one will see many battles along the route to the realization of a vision.

Yes, but we're still defending books like *Slaughterhouse-Five* and *Go Ask Alice*—the very same titles that your school

board called "anti-American, anti-Christian, anti-Semitic, and just plain filthy" when you were a teen.

I'm not surprised. Did racism and segregation end in the U.S. following the Emancipation Proclamation and *Brown v. Board of Education*? Let me ask you and your readers a question. Do you think racism was a factor in the books removed in Island Trees? I do. Of the 11 books banned in Island Trees, more than half were written by prominent African American and Puerto Rican American writers. Why?

The bottom line is that no one in the Island Trees community ever complained about any of these books. Members of the Island Trees Board of Education "found" a list of "objectionable" books on a table at a conference that was being held in another part of the state. Then they returned to our community and searched our public school system for those titles. Why were so many books discussing the experiences of minority groups in the U.S. on that original list?

How did you get involved in all this in the first place?

When the books were first removed from my school, I was 16 years old and serving as vice president of the junior class, and I was on the editorial board of the student newspaper. As student council president in my senior year, I was the liaison between the student body and the board of education. I knew all the board members personally and attended board meetings long before the lawsuit was announced.

I frequently visited our public library, and I learned about the book removal from the librarian. I told the librarian that I wanted to mount a challenge to the removal and, from neighbors, learned that the American Library Association had scheduled a meeting locally, which I attended. I was initially in contact with [lawyer] William Kunstler and the law firm of Ramsey Clark. Later, I decided that the NYCLU (New York Civil Liberties Union) was best suited to carry a case through the courts. I was the sole plaintiff. When the ACLU (American Civil Liberties) Union lawyers approached me about making the lawsuit into a class action, I recommended other students to add their names to the filing.

What motivated you to do it?

I felt I could make a difference. For me, censorship was not simply a right-wing vs. left-wing issue, and I tried my best to frame the debate on censorship my own way. I believe censorship is offensive to the vast majority of Americans, offensive to Americans from the right, offensive to Americans from the center, and offensive to Americans from the left.

Did you realize the importance of it all at the time? Did you realize you'd make history?

Yes and yes. Win or lose, I believed it was a historic battle.

Were you ever scared?

Never. My parents heard from anonymous callers who said I would not receive scholarships for college if I pursued the case, and obviously my parents were concerned. I recall one teacher who whispered to me, "You are doing the right thing." It troubled me that most adults, including my teachers, felt the need to whisper their support.

Were your classmates supportive?

At school, most of the student body—perhaps 85 percent or more—didn't support my position against book banning or were apathetic, so I took matters into my own hands and, alone, I approached the American Library Association for help in finding the best lawyers.

Why didn't more teens and teachers at your school back you?

High school students and their families are preoccupied with getting into colleges, and most people fear involvement in controversial issues. Teachers were worried about tenure and their jobs, since the Board of Education was also their employer.

Would things be different if the case took place today?

Young people today are more informed, mature, and aware of their constitutional rights. There's even a band "Pico vs. Island Trees," which named itself after me, so I'm convinced young people are more involved than ever in change.

Who tends to ban?

Many diverse groups and individuals—from both the majority and the minority—advocate some form of censorship. That does not anger me so much as it scares me. I've encountered feminists who advocate censorship and religious groups advocating censorship, and African-Americans who raise objections to *The Adventures of Huckleberry Finn* and *Gone with the Wind*. This is a very complex issue.

Are book banners motivated by the same things now as they were back then?

I've long assumed most book banners are well-intentioned individuals who wish to protect children. Their method is unconstitutional and incompatible with life in a pluralistic nation. Does ignorance protect children or does ignorance leave young people unprepared and defenseless?

Give us an idea of how long this consumed your life.

I launched the lawsuit at a news conference with Kurt Vonnegut in 1977, when I was president of the Island Trees High School Student Council. In 1981, I received my B.A. from Haverford College, and one year later the Supreme Court handed down its 1982 decision in the Pico case.

What was the most difficult part of going through the lengthy case?

The hard part of going through a long battle is the time taken away from other pursuits. During my first semester at Haverford College, I spent 50 percent of my weekends traveling to other parts of the country to raise awareness about the dangers of censorship.

Why does book banning set a dangerous precedent?

In 1983, on the day commemorating the 50th anniversary of the burning of books in Nazi Germany, I gave a speech in New York against the banning and burning of books. During the 1970s and 1980s, when I was very active battling censorship, *The Diary of Anne Frank* was being removed from shelves by censors here in this country. Need I say more?

Is it ever justified to ban a book in a school or library?

No. Well, the longer answer is there is one instance I can think of when a court may remove a book from public schools. Since the 1947 Court ruling in *Everson v. Board of Education,* even local government is forbidden from actions respecting an "establishment of religion." The First Amendment clause against establishment of religion was intended, in Thomas Jefferson's words, to erect "a wall of separation between church and state." Therefore, possibly, a future court *may* have an obligation to remove a book from a public school system if the book's presence is found to represent an establishment of religion. That would be the sole instance, in my opinion, where a court *may* have to accept a book removal because the prohibition against the establishment of religion comes from within the First Amendment itself. I can foresee no other situation where book removal might be justified in the U.S.

Why does free speech matter?

The First Amendment was the *first* amendment for a reason. Freedom of speech, freedom of inquiry, and the protection of minority views form the foundation of the United States.

What impact did the case have on you as a teen and as an adult?

Then and now, I feel so proud to say, "There was one time in my life when I refused to compromise." The stakes were high, and the political landscape was shifting: the legal battle began during the Carter Administration and ended during the Reagan Administration. The battle was so involved and long that I received my B.A. from Haverford College in between.

You've told me that you didn't want this case to define who you were. What did you mean by that?

You're referring to my comment that, "I didn't wish to become a First Amendment Junkie." I wanted to get those books back on the shelves so public school students and teachers might choose to read and discuss them. Fame held little interest to me, so I turned down opportunities to have a movie made about my life and to sign book deals. During a battle, it's most important to remain focused on the objective.

Do today's kids feel as passionate about free speech as you did?

Personally, I believe more young people are informed and passionate about their rights, and responsibilities to stand up despite the cost, today than at any previous time in American history. I'm sure some of your readers may disagree with that statement. I am simply voicing one opinion, and that is the point, isn't it? The crux is one's freedom to voice an opinion; the crux is one's responsibility to stand up to others who try to silence authors, to silence the dissemination of ideas, to silence librarians, to silence discussion, to silence teachers, to silence students, and to silence the constitutional right to disagree.

Do you think free speech is becoming more important in this age of technology?

Yes, and that's an excellent question, a question others can answer far better than I. I'm a simple guy: I feel Americans should feel encouraged when a young person picks up any book to read.

Periodical and Internet Sources Bibliography

The following articles have been selected to supplement the diverse views presented in this chapter.

Alexandra Alter, "Book Bans Rising Rapidly in the U.S., Free Speech Groups Find," *New York Times*, April 20, 2023. https://www.nytimes.com/2023/04/20/books/book-bans-united-states-free-speech.html.

Porter Anderson, "A US Court Temporarily Blocks a Library and Bookstore Law," *Publishing Perspectives*, July 30, 2023. publishingperspectives.com/2023/07/a-us-court-temporarily-blocks-a-library-and-bookstore-law.

Anthony Aycock, "The largely forgotten book ban case that went up to the Supreme Court," *Washington Post*, May 20, 2023. www.washingtonpost.com/history/2023/05/20/book-bans-supreme-court-pico.

Charles Bethea, "Why Some Florida Schools Are Removing Books from Their Libraries," the *New Yorker*, February 7, 2023. www.newyorker.com/news/letter-from-the-south/why-some-florida-schools-are-removing-books-from-their-libraries.

Suzanne Eckes, "Where the Supreme Court stands on banning books," the *Conversation*, October 2, 2023. theconversation.com/where-the-supreme-court-stands-on-banning-books-212497.

Maddie Hanna, "Is Pennridge secretly banning books? This dad went to court to find out," *Philly Inquirer*, October 8, 2023. www.inquirer.com/education/pennridge-school-district-book-ban-sexualized-content-soft-censoring-20231008.html.

Elizabeth A. Harris and Alexandra Alter, "Authors and Students Sue Over Florida Law Driving Book Bans," *New York Times*, June 20, 2023. www.nytimes.com/2023/06/20/books/book-bans-florida-tango-makes-three.html.

Elizabeth A. Harris and Alexandra Alter, "A Fast-Growing Network of Conservative Groups Is Fueling a Surge in Book Bans," *New York Times*, December 12, 2022. www.nytimes.com/2022/12/12/books/book-bans-libraries.html.

Sarah Mervosh, "The College Board Says A.P. Psychology Is 'Effectively Banned' in Florida," *New York Times*, August 3, 2023. www.nytimes.com/2023/08/03/us/florida-ap-psychology-courses.html.

Brooke Park, "A Federal Court Will Rule on Book Bans in Llano. Many in the Community Have Already Made Up Their Minds," *Texas Monthly*, December 22, 2022. www.texasmonthly.com/news-politics/llano-library-book-bans-lawsuit.

Erik Sandoval, "Battle over Lake County children's picture book ban heard in federal court," WKMG-TV, July 26, 2023. www.clickorlando.com/news/investigators/2023/07/26/battle-over-lake-county-childrens-picture-book-ban-heard-in-federal-court.

Kelly Weill, "Appeals Court Gives Texas Book Ban Law the Green Light," *Daily Beast*, September 26, 2023. www.thedailybeast.com/texas-judges-give-book-ban-law-the-green-light.

OPPOSING VIEWPOINTS® SERIES

Chapter 3

Is Book Banning Good for Education?

Chapter Preface

It's easy, perhaps, to forget that the question of what books students are reading in schools is not necessarily a question with a clear or decisive answer. After all, somebody is tasked with deciding what material should or should not be made available to students, at least in the public forum that is a school, be it teachers, parents, or politicians.

On the one hand, there's the textbook, a seemingly inventive idea that involves compiling texts and ideas together in order to tell a cohesive narrative that's aimed at giving students a sense of what they're trying to learn. But choosing what goes in a textbook has become a debate in itself, with school boards around the country fighting over how much students need to know and what parts of a country's history it is essential to remember. For some, it's the major victories that need to be engrained in the minds of youth; for others, it's the great shames of national history that need to be remembered so that they are never repeated.

But there are other considerations at play too. For some educators, it's also important that children in a multicultural society are exposed to stories that reflect the reality of that life, especially because so much of the so-called literary canon often had been written from the perspective of white men. For some teachers, the classroom can be a place to use the world of books to contradict that commonly told narratives and give a diverse body of students stories that they can see themselves in.

Of course, for others, it's those very books that need to be kept out of schools because they reflect a changing demographic landscape that feels unfamiliar to parents who went to school a generation ago. Few things are ever as frightening as the unfamiliar, though the debate itself can feel as old as time.

Viewpoint 1

> *"For several years, there has been much debate about what is included in school textbooks across the United States. Some readers are dissatisfied with the content of these books due to the composition of the panels that select it."*

How Schools Decide Which Textbooks to Use

Tagari Publications

Banning classic literature isn't the only way that state and local governments can try to control what kind of information students are given in classes. In this excerpted viewpoint, Bobby Tagari *takes a look at some of the longstanding debates about using textbooks in classrooms and, more pointedly, the debate over what goes in them. Dating to the nineteenth century, textbooks were often thought to be one of the most valuable ways to collect information and present that information to students, but they're also a locus point in arguments about what kind of information should be taught to young, potentially impressionable, minds. This viewpoint outlines some of the ways in which these textbooks are selected along with the controversies that accompany this selection process. In particular, this viewpoint considers the process of textbook selection in states like Texas and how this process demonstrates the ways in which politics impact the types*

"The People and Organizations Who Decide What Books Public School Students Read in The United States," by Bobby Tagari, February 9, 2022.

of materials that are included in texbooks. Bobby Tagari *is the blog of an Australian company called Tagari Publications.*

As you read, consider the following questions:

1. Who decides what kinds of textbooks are used in schools?
2. What are some of the pros and cons of basing a curriculum on textbooks?
3. What have been some of the major controversies over what goes into textbooks?

In the United States, the books that are chosen for public schools are decided upon by a variety of people and organizations. The main people who make these decisions are teachers, librarians, school administrators, and parents. There are also many different organizations, such as the National Council of Teachers of English, that have a hand in deciding which books are appropriate for public school students.

The school decides which books to use in each district. The United States has 20 states and three territories, known as textbook adoption states, in total. A small number of schools and school districts provide librarians and classroom teachers with funds to purchase books. They save money because they are more efficient and can be accessed quickly in schools. Education is governed by federal laws and regulations, according to the federal government. In the United States, educational resources are primarily the responsibility of the states and local governments. It is up to the state to pass education laws. States have a significant influence on the curriculum selection, development, and regulation of public schools.

The state board establishes a framework for each discipline that outlines the goals, minimum standards, and content that must be covered in each course. After that, a committee of volunteers reviews and selects textbooks from the library.

The state makes its textbooks decisions through one of two methods. Thirty states, along with the District of Columbia, allow local governments and schools to select textbooks. In addition to 20 states and three territories, known as textbook adoption states, each state and territory has its own set of textbooks.

[...]

The Pros and Cons of Textbook Adoption

In recent years, there has been a growing movement toward incorporating various types of instructional materials into the classroom, with various groups of people arguing about how to do so. Textbooks have long been regarded as an important educational resource, and their use as a substitute for more experienced teachers has become increasingly common.

For instance, in Texas, the Texas Board of Education (SBOE) decides which instructional materials to use in the state's classrooms. A textbook, software package, or other learning tool is graded on a one-to-one basis by the SBOE, and each must be given a score of 50 percent or higher to be adopted. They conduct a review of the materials' coverage of the TEKS [Texas Essential Knowledge and Skills] for their subject as well as any potentially troublesome content.

California, Florida, and Texas are the three states that have experienced the greatest increase in textbook adoption in recent years. According to a White House report, the textbook market is estimated to be worth $7-8 billion, with California, Florida, and Texas being the most effective states in implementing it. The reason for this high price is most likely due to the large number of schools in these states and the high number of students who use textbooks.

Who Determines Which Textbooks to Use in a Classroom?

There is no one answer to this question as it can vary depending on the school, district, or state. In some cases, the decision may be made by the individual teacher, while in others it may be made at the district level by a committee. Ultimately, the goal is to choose textbooks that are aligned with the state's educational standards and that will provide students with the information and skills they need to be successful.

Many public schools incorporate the curriculum from the textbook into their history and social studies classes. The state's standards, curriculums, laws, and textbook review panels all play a role in how the education system is governed. Textbook content is frequently heavily influenced by political ideology. The Texas panel consisted of educators, parents, business representatives, and a Christian pastor and politician.

State educational standards necessitate that many K-12 teachers adhere to these standards. Texas has approximately 5 million public school students, making it one of the largest states in the country. It has an undue influence on national textbook publishers and their content, which it does not include. When it comes to selecting history textbooks, many people have their own political agendas. If students are only taught a one-dimensional history of the United States, they will be unable to change it for the better.

It's clear that state adoption processes can help teachers select the best textbooks for their classrooms. They will be able to meet state requirements if their books are aligned with state standards and meet state regulations pertaining to a wide range of subjects. It is critical to note that not all books are appropriate for every classroom setting.

Who Set the School Curriculum?

There is no one answer to this question as it varies from school to school. In some cases, the school board or district may set the curriculum, while in others the teachers may have more autonomy. Some schools may also use a mix of both standardized curriculum and teacher-created lesson plans.

For instance, in Washington, the administrators of the Grandview School District spent $200,000 developing their own curriculum. Six years ago, only 13 percent of sophomores passed state math exams; now, 64 percent do. In addition to the curriculum, a district shares instructional resources with other districts, which is known as an open educational resource (OER). Teachers now have the option of publishing and selling their own curriculum materials online. Teachers can sell original classroom material such as lesson plans, games, and other resources on the marketplace. By creating its own curriculum, a Pennsylvania school district saved at least $300,000 on textbook purchases. Teachers used the CK-12 Foundation, a free online library of textbooks, videos, and lessons, to create their own materials. As part of #GoOpen, the district has joined the ranks of six education departments that have adopted this campaign.

Despite its proponents' claims that the National Curriculum is prescriptive and does not allow for enough creativity or freedom of expression, some critics argue that it does so. They also contend that adjusting to the academic requirements can be difficult, and that if they do not fit in with the curriculum, it can be difficult for them to find a place in the classroom.

There is no law requiring private schools in the United States to adhere to the national curriculum. They are free to select the curriculum that best suits their needs. It allows them to choose whether to follow the national curriculum, as they do at many state schools, or to deviate from it entirely.

There is no national curriculum test available in the United States. Throughout the course, each teacher organizes his or her own exams, classes, and exams for each term (finals) and mid-term (mid-terms) half-way through a term. The weight of the term grade is determined by the method of testing or quizzing.

This method of learning works well for the vast majority of students because it enables them to learn at their own pace. However, some students may find it difficult to adjust to a flexible system and feel lost or impoverished if they are unable to fit into the traditional curriculum.

[...]

Who Decides What Goes in History Textbooks?

In the United States, state and local officials decide which textbooks to use in public schools. Private schools can choose any textbook they want. Publishers usually send textbook samples to state and local officials to try to get their books adopted.

There are no national historical or civics standards in the United States. Every state develops its own set of criteria for what students should study in social studies. Politics and civic values have long played a role in determining what children learn. States have significant influence over the standards for history and social studies. Despite the fact that there are numerous variations in the number of standards that are in place, it is impossible to predict how many will be in place in the future. For instance, students in North Carolina are required by new standards to examine U.S. history as a way to learn about discrimination.

According to the Thomas B. Fordham Institute, states with higher standards received high marks. The last time national standards for history were reviewed was almost three decades ago. Social studies literacy is also covered as part of the common-core standards. The College Board revised the AP U.S. History framework in 2012. Although each state establishes its own guidelines for general high school history courses, AP teachers follow the same guidelines. To prepare students for K-12 education, educators should look to the Roadmap to Educating for American Democracy for historical and civic lessons. Its guiding document emphasizes the concept of reflective patriotism.

Different states' standards require that different types of content be covered. Depending on the state, the same textbook can tell vastly different stories. Social studies is a crowded field, and determining which materials are being used by teachers can be difficult. At the very least, there isn't a lot of external scrutiny of social studies materials, but there is a lot of evaluation data for other subjects. Each school system makes its own decision as to what content to teach its students. Eleven states have enacted legislation requiring schools to limit how racist and sexist comments can be discussed in class. What effects will the new laws have on the selection and use of materials?

There's no easy way to know for sure. Materials have already been challenged under one of the new state laws. Moms for Liberty tested four books as part of the Wit and Wisdom English/language arts curriculum. The group was dissatisfied with the books' message, which they believed was that all white people were evil. According to the educational organization Great Minds, there are no curricular materials that teach Critical Race Theory, despite groups like Moms for Liberty claiming otherwise. At local school board meetings, it is common for people to express their dissatisfaction and cause changes in instruction. For instance, a Pennsylvania district withdrew a donation of books after parents complained about the use of critical race theory in the classroom. However, in many cases, local school boards have no authority to change state standards.

Controversy Over Textbook Content in the United States

For several years, there has been much debate about what is included in school textbooks across the United States. Some readers are dissatisfied with the content of these books due to the composition of the panels that select it. As a result of Texas' large market, the approval process for textbooks is significantly more time-consuming than in other states. Publishers want their books to be approved in Texas because it means that the country as a whole will be more likely to buy them. Some people believe that the content chosen for this process is inappropriate for younger students, which has been a source of contention for some time. According to the Texas State Board of Education, the textbooks they have approved should represent the state's curriculum, and they are defending their decision to approve them.

Public School Textbooks

Public school textbooks are designed to give students a well-rounded education in a variety of subjects. While they are not always the most up-to-date or comprehensive texts available, they provide a solid foundation for learning. In recent years, there has been an increased focus on using public school textbooks to teach critical thinking and analytical skills, rather than simply rote memorization. This shift is aimed at better preparing students for the challenges they will face in the real world.

Textbooks were thought to be the most valuable tools in the nineteenth century by educators. Textbooks contributed to the definition of acceptable knowledge and the design of instruction. Among the most well-known high school textbook authors of this era were New England-born Protestant, white men and New England-educated white women. These voices of authority instilled in talented young people a sense of intellectual and moral superiority. The laws of science, in addition to helping legitimize a society whose economic system favored growth and man's dominion over nature, served as a foundation for it. According to educators, science also taught logic, as well as helped sharpen observation skills. In chemistry texts from high school, students were promised practical education that showed how a benevolent God worked.

Who Determines the Content of Textbooks

There is no one answer to this question as it can vary depending on the country, state, or district. In some cases, the textbook publisher may have some input on the content of the textbook. However, the main people who determine the content of textbooks are usually the teachers and educators who will be using them.

This article investigates how public and professional participation is measured in textbook selection processes in various states. Despite the fact that centralized adoption provides a forum for citizens and interest groups to present competing cultural and symbolic claims, it has a limited impact on professional educators, according to the report.

The process of how textbooks are selected and who gets to select them is constantly in flux. As a result, the type of material included in textbooks and school curricula is also regularly subject to change. For instance, publishers in Texas have been asked by the state to remove instructional materials from textbooks based on district curriculum over the last few years. In this policy change, the state believes that textbooks should be uniform throughout the state, and that instructional materials that differ from the prescribed course of study should be removed.

This policy change has sparked some debate because it eliminates any educational motive from the text, with the emphasis being placed on prescribed standards instead. As a result of the policy change, some publishers have removed political statements from their textbooks.

This change is unpopular, but it stems from the belief that textbooks should be uniform across the state. The syllabus should be properly integrated with the previous class's and the previous class's tests. As a result, students are prepared to take the upcoming tests.

[…]

Viewpoint 3

> *"Bedtime stories aren't just lovely endings to the day or a way to induce sleep, they are also a safe way to experience and discuss all sorts of feelings and situations."*

The Importance of Diversity in Children's Literature

BJ Woodstein

In this viewpoint, BJ Woodstein makes the case for maintaining some control over what books kids are reading. Woodstein thinks an active effort needs to be made in order for them to read diverse stories. In a multicultural society, she writes that it's essential that students and young children see themselves reflected in the stories that they read. She argues that doing so is useful for giving glimpses into what their adult lives will look like and eradicating the emotional experience of prejudice. Woodstein argues that it is detrimental that the characters in so many classic tales remain very white and male. BJ Woodstein is an associate professor of literature and translation at the University of East Anglia, which is located in Norwich, England.

"Why children's books that teach diversity are more important than ever," by BJ Woodstein, The Conversation, February 6, 2017. https://theconversation.com/why-childrens-books-that-teach-diversity-are-more-important-than-ever-72146.

As you read, consider the following questions:

1. Why does Woodstein say that children's books can act like both mirrors and windows to the world?
2. What is behind what the writer calls "a sense of false nostalgia?"
3. According to data cited in this viewpoint, what percentage of characters in children's literature are white?

If you think back to your childhood, what sticks with you? For many people, it's those cosy times when they were cuddled up with a parent or grandparent, being read a story.

But bedtime stories aren't just lovely endings to the day or a way to induce sleep, they are also a safe way to experience and discuss all sorts of feelings and situations. So even when children think they're just being told about an adorable bunny's adventures, they are actually learning about the world around them.

We know that children's books can act like both mirrors and windows on the world. Mirrors in that they can reflect on children's own lives, and windows in that they can give children a chance to learn about someone else's life. We also know that this type of self-reflection and opportunity to read or hear about different lives is essential for young people.

Research on prejudice shows that coming in contact with people who are different—so-called "others"—helps to reduce stereotypes. This is because when we see people who initially seem different, we learn about them and get closer to them through their story. The "other" seems less far away and, well, less "otherly."

But while it may be ideal for children to actually meet people from different backgrounds in person, if that isn't possible, books can serve as a first introduction to an outside world.

Representing the World

Despite knowing how important it is for diversity to be represented in our day-to-day lives, many children's books are still littered with white, male, able-bodied, heterosexual, cisgender, nominally Christian characters. And research suggests that over 80% of characters in children's books are white—which clearly doesn't reflect the reality of our world.

All of these reasons are why the We Need Diverse Books movement was set in motion in 2014, stemming from a discussion between children's books authors Ellen Oh and Malinda Lo. The movement aims for more diverse children's books to actually be created and for these works to be available to young people. And while we need people to actually write them, we also need publishers to produce them, and bookstores, libraries, and schools to stock them.

As someone who researches children's literature, I think we'd have fewer conflicts in the world if we all read more diverse literature and lived more diverse lives.

I like to think that if we had more diverse children's books, featuring a broad range of characters in many different jobs and situations, as well as more diverse role models in the media, young people would feel empowered, and they'd believe that when they grow up, they could be anyone and do anything they wanted. And they'd look at their friends and think the same for them, and they'd grow up respecting and appreciating everyone's talents.

With this mindset present, issues such as race or religion wouldn't even play a subconscious role. And it would mean that within a generation or two, we wouldn't read articles about appalling and depressing statistics, and we wouldn't need campaigns to increase diversity in literature, academia, or anywhere else.

Role Models

But books aren't just about "others". When we see people like ourselves in the media, including in fiction, we get a glimpse of who we might become, and we feel validated. We can gain role models and inspiration through literature.

Perhaps partly in response to people's growing awareness of the need for role models—whether in person or in literature—one young black girl, Marley Dias, started a campaign to find 1,000 "black girl books." Dias recommends works such as *Brown Girl Dreaming* by Jacqueline Woodson, *One Crazy Summer* by Rita Williams-Garcia, *Chains* by Laurie Halse Anderson and *I Love My Hair* by Natasha Anastasia Tarpley.

But I wonder how many of those "black girl books" feature black girls in prominent roles, such as working as professors, doctors, teachers, or even as presidents of nations. I have a suspicion that the percentage would be disappointingly low.

Just featuring a minority character isn't enough to create quality diverse literature, but it is a first step. And while there are some useful websites that recommend diverse children's books and even literary awards dedicated to promoting such works, much still needs to be done.

Along with the increased worries today about immigrants, refugees, and general "otherness," some societies seem to be headed towards a sense of false nostalgia about a time when the world was controlled by whites.

Given this is not how the world is or should be, we owe it to young readers to show them reality in the books they're reading. Perhaps then the next generation will be less frightened of the "other" if they get to meet them and learn about them from an early age.

Viewpoint 3

> *"Anxieties have not been helped by political leaders who capitalize on the opportunity to politicize the school curriculum for the purposes of leveraging their opponents and stoking their bases."*

Book Bans Are a Political Tool

Alex Bacalja

In this viewpoint, Alex Bacalja takes a look at the way that political debates skew conversations about what children are reading. Because these books later become the ones that shape many children's education, there's a significant collective stake in what those books are. This also means that elected officials often have reason to weigh in and rile up their voter bases. And the issue isn't only one that's animating politics in the U.S.—in this viewpoint, Bacalja is actually talking about the cultural war over book banning in Australia, which indicates that this issue is widespread. Wherever people are reading books, a debate awaits about what exactly it is that they should be reading. Alex Bacalja is a lecturer at the Melbourne Graduate School of Education, which is part of the University of Melbourne.

"'Nostalgic' classics, or edgy contemporary texts? What books are kids reading in Australian schools – and does it matter?," by Alex Bacalja, The Conversation, January 29, 2023. https://theconversation.com/nostalgic-classics-or-edgy-contemporary-texts-what-books-are-kids-reading-in-australian-schools-and-does-it-matter-198234.

As you read, consider the following questions:

1. What is the connection that the author sees between compulsory education and the current debate over banning books in schools?
2. Why is there an almost total lack of opportunity for students to read and study digital forms of literary work?
3. What are the different ways students can be taught to read, according to this viewpoint?

Debates about what books students should be reading in high school reach a crescendo at the start of each school year.

As parents make their way through school text lists, collecting books for their teen's year ahead, they inevitably draw comparisons between their own school reading and the literature selected for their children by teachers, schools and mandated curriculum.

Some are astounded their teens are still reading the same books they read at school.

Everyone Has an Opinion

One father of a Year 9 daughter wondered on Twitter last week, at the start of the 2023 school year, why she was assigned the "boring" *Animal Farm, Romeo and Juliet* and *Wuthering Heights*. (His original post was so flooded with responses, he became overwhelmed and deleted it.)

Some of his fellow parents agreed an all-classics diet threatened to turn teens off reading, and called for older texts to be replaced with contemporary ones that reflected teen lives. Some raised the diversity problem of the so-called—mainly white male—"canon". And others called for a blend of classic and contemporary books, to tick all the boxes.

But everyone had an opinion.

Compulsory schooling has done extraordinary things for our collective skills and knowledge. But one of the consequences of requiring almost everybody to complete a secondary education is that it has become common, even natural, for adults to hold strong beliefs about the "right" kinds of literature that should occupy school time.

In the social media age, it is easier than ever for parents to share these views. Their concerns are also tied up in almost perpetual anxiety about young people and their futures.

Diversity Backlash

These anxieties have not been helped by political leaders who capitalise on the opportunity to politicise the school curriculum for the purposes of leveraging their opponents and stoking their bases. Whenever attempts are made to read and study texts in the English classroom that reflect the diversity of Australian society—and within Australian classrooms—the backlash is intense and sustained.

When former Prime Minister Tony Abbott appointed staunch conservatives to review English in the Australian Curriculum, the resulting report was awash with racist commentary about the "wrong kinds of literature", and called for a greater emphasis on Western literature.

More recently, attempts were made by New South Wales legislative council member Mark Latham to amend the Education Act, so that teachers who taught gender fluidity—including through the selection of texts with gender fluid characters—would be sacked.

These examples demonstrate the precarious grounds upon which teachers must make decisions about which literature is best for their students.

What Are They Reading at School?

Concerningly, no research has ever been conducted in Australia to collect reliable data about what a typical high-school reading list contains. This means almost all of the discussion about the content of teen reading in schools is based on observations, anecdotes and presumptions.

We do have a good sense of what students might be *taught*.

The Australian Curriculum, along with the various state iterations of that guiding document, makes suggestions about the types of literature students should be exposed to: classic and contemporary world literature, including texts from and about Asia and First Nations people. And about the forms literature should take: novels, poetry, short stories and plays; fiction for young adults and children, multimodal texts such as film, and a variety of nonfiction.

However, specific titles are not identified in these documents. Senior (Years 11 and 12) English and Literature curricula across Australian states and territories provide more guidance, with most jurisdictions providing highly restrictive lists from which teachers must select texts for their classes.

Some of the limited evidence we have from the past and present suggests we have a long way to go to produce reading lists that reflect contemporary realities. For example, Demond Gibbs studied the content and use of school books in Victoria between 1848-1948.

The early School Papers (1896-1928) tended to privilege British content, reflected conservative social views, were Royalist in tone, and included a small selection of Australian authors. The 1928 shift to the Victorian Reader, a series of eight books commissioned by the Victorian Education Department, reflected a strong sense of Australian nationalism and far less emphasis on empire. Titles included: *John and Betty*, *Playmates*, and *Holidays*.

More recent research suggests "traditional" literary texts remain the bedrock of senior school reading. One study of ten years of Victorian Senior English texts lists found Indigenous literature is rarely included in these lists and prescribed lists don't reflect our diverse society. Almost 10% of all texts listed are from the writing of William Shakespeare, John Donne, Percy Bysshe Shelley, Charles Dickens, Charlotte and Emily Bronte, and Ernest Hemingway.

Another study reported that in New South Wales, the recycling of "the same old texts"—like *Great Expectations*—is common practice, and others concluded the teaching of Australian literature is inconsistent.

Research also suggests there is an almost total lack of opportunity for students to read and study digital forms of literary work in the senior years of schooling.

It appears those lamenting the death of the classics have nothing to fear.

What Does It Matter?

Given we don't really know what students are reading in schools, and the world has continued turning on its axis, does this really matter?

On the one hand, it matters greatly. Schools have a powerful role: consecrating some stories and knowledges at the expense of others. As renowned French sociologist Pierre Bourdieu established across decades of research, schools and education systems are fundamental tools of state. They actively contribute to the production of certain types of "cultivated" people.

The inclusion and exclusion of literary works is just one way this tool operates. This cultivating has its foundations in ideas about so-called classics.

Arguing about the texts teens will read at school is a perfect example of what Emeritus Professor Bill Green calls "the representation" problem.

Since we cannot fit the entire world into the classroom, we must use the curriculum to select which forms of life to represent. Discrimination is inevitable and always political. This discrimination is evident in decision-making about which children's picture books receive awards, just as much as controversies about narrowly selected judging panels for adult literary awards.

Adding all texts and all textual modes to school reading lists is impossible. The challenge is for teachers and other stakeholders to be honest about the current state of affairs and priorities—and to also reflect on what might be missing and in need of attention.

Australian schools have been lucky to avoid the waves of book-banning spreading the U.S. The most recent iteration bans African American studies and even the use of the word "gay" in classrooms.

Such bans reflect highly outdated and uninformed views about how children read and the purpose of literature in schooling.

It's Not What They Read, It's How They Read

Another way to approach big questions about reading at school is to focus less on what is selected, and more on how these texts will be taught.

The conflation of literature and literacy has meant the content of school reading has contributed to an ignorance, at least outside school staff rooms and teacher training courses, of the importance of reading pedagogies: the methods of instruction teachers use when modelling and supporting reading at school.

School reading is about much more than the recitation of details related to characters, quotes and story events. The many reading approaches a teacher can deploy makes it difficult for parents or politicians to judge the validity of a particular text selected for study.

These approaches might include, for example, reading for pleasure, reading to explore identity and questions of belonging and alienation, or reading (and writing) to understand social media and the explosion of digital culture.

Despite the failure of standardised tests like NAPLAN to improve school outcomes, and evidence we do not need high-stakes and high-stress exams to determine end-of-year scores for year 12s, the narrow forms of reading dominated by these approaches crowd out space for rich and diverse school reading.

Trust Teachers

We must be honest with each other and recognise we don't really know whether reading literature makes us better people.

I am reminded here of Franco-American literary critic and philosopher George Steiner. He questions the idea high literacy can civilise individuals, by reminding us of those SS officers who would spend their evenings listening to Bach and Schubert and reading

Goethe and Rilke, then go to work at the Auschwitz concentration camp in the mornings.

It would be wonderful if school reading could help heal us, process our emotions and develop empathy.

For now, we must put our faith in English teachers. We must trust them—without interference—to select texts for our teens. They know how literature can support the learning needs of their students better than anyone else. And they have spent their entire working lives specialising in the craft of teaching and supporting reading.

Viewpoint 4

"We believe parents have every right and responsibility to monitor what their children read. But they don't have the right to prevent other children from reading books, particularly national award-winning books."

Why Parents Are Banning Books

Finlo Rohrer

In this viewpoint, Finlo Rohrer explains the issue of book banning in the U.S., offering some of the reasons why parents object to certain types of literature. To many parents involved in the debate over book banning, it is an emotional issue, with some parents angered by the perceived loss of innocence their children experience as a result of reading these books. Rohrer notes that book banning is considerably more common in the U.S. than in the UK for several reasons. Finlo Rohrer is a data and analysis editor for the BBC.

As you read, consider the following questions:

1. What is one factor Rohrer says contributed to the rise in book bans?
2. According to this viewpoint, why are there fewer formal book bans in the UK than in the U.S.?

"Why are parents banning school books?," by Finlo Rohrer, BBC, September 27, 2010.

3. What effect does banning a book have on a child or teen's interest in the book, according to this viewpoint?

There is a battle being fought in America over books.

The skirmishes see concerned parents "challenge" books which are being used in schools.

Other parents are fighting for the right of their children to go into their school library and pick up those very same books.

The issue is being highlighted by the American Library Association during its Banned Books Week.

The ALA recorded 460 attempts in 2009 to have a book withdrawn from a library or classroom.

Part of the problem lies in the rise of young adult fiction. Nearly 60 years after the publication of *The Catcher in the Rye*, teenager readers are now a lucrative market around the world.

The *Twilight* series has brought author Stephenie Meyer millions, but she has also found her work in the top 10 most challenged, with parents objecting to sexual explicitness and unsuitability for younger readers.

More surprising to many people would be the three established literary classics on the list. The 10 most challenged include *The Catcher in the Rye*, *The Color Purple* and even *To Kill A Mockingbird*.

"I was shocked that anybody would find this book offensive," says Barbara Jones, director of the office for intellectual freedom at the ALA.

Harper Lee's book has been challenged by black parents who object to the use of the word "n**ger." It appears 58 times in the book, notes Ms. Jones.

But for most challenged books, the issue is usually sex or sexuality.

Lauren Myracle has endured a stream of angry e-mails from parents who are outraged by her bestselling series about a group of teenage girls. They are all written in the style of instant messaging, and the three books are called *ttyl*, *ttfn* and *l8r, g8r*.

"It is so revealing to me the vituperativeness they address me with. They are angry," she says.

A typical e-mail reads: "What gives you the right to take away my child's innocence?"

"I've got one teenager who has got a potty mouth," says Myracle. "These are high school girls, one is trying to decide whether to have sex with her boyfriend."

Many of the challenges recorded by the ALA are aimed at high-schools, restricting the reading material of children aged 14-18.

But even books for younger readers, like Myracle's work *Twelve*, can generate floods of complaints. The book describes a girl figuring out how to put in a tampon, which prompted angry e-mails.

Myracle argues that to engage with teenagers you need to write honestly about them.

"Kids need to see their world reflected back to them. I've had many girls say thank you for writing this."

There's a disparity between the US and UK. While in the US, formal challenges to books in school libraries are routine, they are very unusual in the UK.

Part of the difference is in the level of local control over schools. Typically in the US, locally-elected school boards can have books withdrawn when parents petition them.

In the UK, control lies almost exclusively in the hands of headteachers, says Sally Duncan, of the School Library Association. She can recall one primary school that refused to have any *Harry Potter* books because of the supernatural content, but such moves are rare.

"Parents are perhaps less likely to complain about the content of books in the UK as, by and large, we are a less 'religious' society," says Ms Duncan.

Across the Atlantic, one struggle has been played out in the small town of Stockton, Missouri, over Sherman Alexie's book *The Absolutely True Diary of a Part-Time Indian.*

The work has won a National Book Award, but the story of a 14-year-old Native American on a poverty-stricken reservation,

The Politics of Book Banning

It appears that public libraries are another battleground for the United States' ever-present culture wars.

- Another 41% of titles challenged or banned have content relating to LGBTQIA+ identity and themes, according to PEN.
- This dynamic has existed for decades. Famed novelist Judy Blume faced heavy scrutiny and calls for censorship in the 1980s for her books that discussed sexuality and self-image.
- The number one banned book is once again *Gender Queer* by Maia Kobabe, a graphic memoir that follows Kobabe's journey into exploring their own gender and queer identity.

What Are People Saying?

In his re-election video released on Tuesday, Joe Biden cited books as part of the "bedrock freedoms" under threat by "MAGA extremists." Here's what he said at a White House event honoring educators earlier this week:

> I never thought I'd be a president who is fighting against elected officials trying to ban, and banning, books.

Lessa Kanani'opua Pelayo-Lozada, president of the American Library Association, on how the campaign for books being banned has ramped up in past years:

> Now we're seeing organized attempts by groups to censor multiple titles throughout the country without actually having read many of these books.

Elle Mehltretter, a 16-year-old who spoke with NPR's Tovia Smith about circumventing book bans online in her home state of Florida:

> You can say you ban books all you want, but you can never really ban them because they're everywhere.

So, What Now?

- Grassroots organizers from all walks of life are responding. Take those putting banned books in Little Free Libraries, or organizing banned book giveaways.
- Earlier last year, the Brooklyn Public Library announced a program allowing free online access to any of their available "banned" titles.
- The battle for books continues in places like Llano, Texas, where county commissioners recently held a meeting to decide whether they should close their public library system entirely instead of restoring 17 banned titles upon the orders of a federal judge.

"Book bans are getting everyone's attention — including Biden's. Here's why," by Manuela López Restrepo, National Public Radio Inc. (NPR), April 25, 2023.

touched by tragedy, upset many parents in Stockton after they learned it was being used in lessons in the school.

The opposition to the book was led by lawyer and parent Mike Holzknecht.

"The book is just chock full of vulgarity, profanity, obscenity and sexual explicitness involving minors," he says. "People around here, where it's pretty rural and conservative, they will go a long way, but this book was so far over the edge. It doesn't belong in a school."

After a number of meetings spread over several months, the book's opponents succeeded. The school board voted to withdraw the book from the school curriculum and the school library.

Cheryl Marcum was among those who were defending the book.

"It was one of the best books I've ever read in my life. The themes are pervasive poverty, alcoholism, bullying, racism and absolutely no hope. All of that applies to Cedar County [where Stockton is].

"We believe parents have every right and responsibility to monitor what their children read. But they don't have the right to prevent other children from reading books, particularly national award-winning books."

Mr. Holzknecht accepts the book is a "nice story" but can't accept the language or the sexual explicitness. He moved his family to Stockton because he felt it was a place with good, shared values.

"This is a community with the type of values that are consistent with the way we like to raise our children." Why are parents banning school books?

The fundamental split is between those who think teachers should be able to challenge and engage children with edgy books, and those who think only the parents should be allowed to do that.

"We are overprotecting our children," suggests Ms. Jones. "They have heard this language. They have probably said it themselves. It isn't dangerous for children to be able to confront unpleasant ideas. What better place to engage with ideas than in a school or in a library?"

And of course the net result of a battle over a book, like Stockton's, is that more children end up reading the suddenly controversial work and the author sells more books. Even Mr. Holzknecht has to admit he's purchased three copies.

"These boards are fooling themselves that if they ban the book the kids aren't going to get hold of them," says Ms. Jones.

To kids, contraband is cool.

Periodical and Internet Sources Bibliography

The following articles have been selected to supplement the diverse views presented in this chapter.

Ta-Nehisi Coates, "The Case of the Fallacious Textbook," the *Atlantic*, January 3, 2011. www.theatlantic.com/national/archive/2011/01/the-case-of-the-fallacious-textbook/68780.

Ella Creamer, "'Eating away at democracy': book bans in US public schools rise by a third in a year," the *Guardian*, September 22, 2023. www.theguardian.com/books/2023/sep/22/democracy-book-bans-us-public-schools-rise.

Melissa Gira Grant, "Conservatives Are Trying to Ban Books in Your Town. Librarians Are Fighting Back," the *New Republic*, March 16, 2023. newrepublic.com/article/170920/conservative-book-bans-libraries-fighting-back.

Dana Goldstein, "I Read 4,800 Pages of American History Textbooks," *New York Times*, January 13, 2020. www.nytimes.com/2020/01/13/reader-center/american-history-textbooks-journalism.html.

Dana Goldstein, "Two States. Eight Textbooks. Two American Stories," *New York Times*, January 12, 2020. www.nytimes.com/interactive/2020/01/12/us/texas-vs-california-history-textbooks.html.

Dana Goldstein and Stephanie Saul, "A Look Inside the Textbooks That Florida Rejected," *New York Times*, April 22, 2022. www.nytimes.com/2022/04/22/us/florida-rejected-textbooks.html.

Elise Hannum, "What Book Bans Take from Kids," the *Atlantic*, September 23, 2022. www.theatlantic.com/books/archive/2022/09/books-briefing-zora-neale-hurston-lemony-snicket/671504.

Marilisa Jiménez Garcia, "Book Bans Are Targeting the History of Oppression," the *Atlantic*, February 2, 2022. https://www.theatlantic.com/family/archive/2022/02/maus-book-ban-tennessee-art-spiegelman/621453/.

E. Tammy Kim, "When the Culture Wars Come for the Public Library," the *New Yorker,* April 20, 2023. www.newyorker.com/news/dispatch/when-the-culture-wars-come-for-the-public-library.

Valeriya Safronova, "New Russian High School Textbooks Seek to Justify War in Ukraine," *New York Times*, September 1, 2023. www.nytimes.com/2023/09/01/world/europe/russia-textbooks-ukraine-war.html.

Katy Waldman, "What Are We Protecting Children from by Banning Books?," the *New Yorker*, March 10, 2023. www.newyorker.com/books/page-turner/what-are-we-protecting-children-from-by-banning-books.

Annie Julia Wyman, "What Kind of Town Bans Books?," the *New Yorker*, October 1, 2014. www.newyorker.com/books/page-turner/what-kind-of-town-bans-books.

OPPOSING VIEWPOINTS® SERIES

Chapter 4

Is Book Banning Good for Society?

Chapter Preface

Most of the viewpoints in this book so far have looked at the impact banning, limiting, or challenging books has on the students themselves and their education. Another big question is what the impact limiting books has on society writ large.

For some, the philosophy of banning books comes from an effort to create a more ideal society. Arguments supporting this idea come from a place of trying to limit exposure to elements of society that parents and others fear because they are new or different from what they were used to. Other ideas in support of limiting or banning books come from trying to make sure that the books students do read match current social mores. Instead of banning them outright, there have been efforts to rewrite classic literary texts and make them less offensive.

But there's also no reason to limit our examination of the world of banned books to the U.S. and the Western world. Some of the most interesting book bans happen around the world, from countries trying to restrict so-called dangerous information to deeper complaints about the imagery of foreign cultures.

Most supporters behind the idea of limiting the spread of books are picking and choosing which titles cause offense in the hope that such things will be ignored and forgotten about on a large scale. The folks on the other side of the debate, however, take a more holistic approach, arguing that banning one book becomes tantamount to banning all of them.

VIEWPOINT 1

> *"As the push to pass judgment on—and remove—certain books from schools has become a national drive with national attention from conservative and liberal media, tempers have become increasingly frayed."*

The Negative Impact of Book Bans on Education

Anthony Zurcher

In this viewpoint from the BBC on proposed book bans in the U.S., Anthony Zurcher makes the case that students are getting the short end of the stick in terms of limiting the amount of education that they're able to get in schools where these bans have been imposed by parent groups. From this perspective, the debate over what books should and should not be used in schools goes beyond just limiting the general availability of educational resources. It speaks to the overall creation of a culture of fear in schools that some are calling "soft censorship," meaning that teachers are being forced to tread carefully, afraid of stoking the next cultural fight. Zurcher is the BBC's senior North American reporter.

"'Why are certain school books being banned in US?,'" by Anthony Zurcher, BBC, February 7, 2022.

As you read, consider the following questions:

1. Out of the first 100 books that a state legislator in Texas said may cause students to feel "discomfort, guilt, anguish or any other form of psychological distress," how many of them were written by ethnic minorities, women, or LGBTQIA+ authors?
2. Why, according to this viewpoint, do these proposed book bans do significant damage to open discourse and learning across the country?
3. What kinds of rights and agency does this viewpoint say that students should have?

A growing number of U.S. parents are alleging that school books are obscene or otherwise harmful to children. It's creating an increasingly divisive political battle that could spill over into upcoming national elections.

Yael Levin-Sheldon, a mother of two who lives near Richmond, Virginia, recently heard about a book that a teacher in an area school brought into the classroom. She made a note of the title, *The Black Friend: On Being a Better White Person.*

The title alone, Levin says, is racist—and it's not the kind of book that should be available to children in public schools.

"Now think of it saying, 'on being a better black person,'" she said. "Would that be ok?"

Levin-Sheldon is the Virginia chapter president of the conservative parents-rights group No Left Turn in Education. Her organisation compiles a list of books it says are "used to spread radical and racist ideologies to students" and "divide us as a people for the purpose of indoctrinating kids to a dangerous ideology."

The list includes Margaret Atwood's dystopian novel *The Handmaid's Tale* and *White Fragility* by Robin Diangelo. *The Black Friend*, a New York Times best-selling memoir by Frederick Joseph recounting his challenges as a black student in a predominantly white high school, isn't on the list. At least, not yet.

Books such as Joseph's—offering critical views on topics like U.S. history or race—gained new prominence in school curricula and library collections as a response to the Black Lives Matter protests of 2020 and educational efforts to address concerns about persistent racism in the U.S. No Left Turn contends that the works should be taught in context, along with other texts that provide a different (and assumedly more positive) view of America's past. And parents, Levin-Sheldon adds, should have the choice of opting out of those lessons.

Other works, however, particularly ones that touch on human sexuality in explicit detail, should be outright prohibited, the group argues.

"When it comes to pornography and paedophilia," Levin-Sheldon says, "that's when we want those books removed."

This, she adds, is all her group is seeking. It's not too different from what free-speech advocates and educators say they would like, as well—a conversation between parents, teachers and school librarians, balancing moral and educational interests and conducted with the best interests of the children in mind.

In practice, however, it hasn't always worked out that way.

A Rising Tide of Complaints

A state legislator in Texas produced a list of more than 850 books that he contended may cause students to feel "discomfort, guilt, anguish or any other form of psychological distress" because of their race or sex. A *Dallas Morning News* review found 97 of the first 100 books on the list were written by ethnic minorities, women or LGBTQ authors.

A school district in San Antonio pulled 400 of those books from its libraries without any formal review process or specific complaints from parents.

A Tennessee school board removed *Maus*, a Pulitzer Prize-winning graphic novel about the Holocaust, from its eighth-grade curriculum because of profanity and anthropomorphised mouse nudity.

In Polk County, Florida, a school removed 16 books pending review, including award-winning novels *The Kite Runner* by Khaled Hosseini and *Beloved* by Toni Morrison, because they contained "obscene material."

Challenges have come from the left, as well. A school district near Seattle, Washington, dropped the 1960 Harper Lee classic *To Kill a Mockingbird* from its curriculum because of its depiction of race relations and use of racist language.

Characters' use of racist epithets also prompted efforts last year to limit the teaching of John Steinbeck's *Of Mice and Men* in school districts in Mendota Heights, Minnesota, and Burbank, California.

The American Library Association keeps track of the number of complaints lodged against books in school libraries and has recorded a marked increase over the past year. According to preliminary data, from September through November of 2021 the association tallied 330 incidents. The total number reported for all of 2019, the last year schools across the U.S. were in-person for the entire year, was 377—suggesting that the final 2021 numbers ultimately will dwarf previous amounts.

The cumulative effect, says Deborah Caldwell-Stone, director of the association's Office for Intellectual Freedom, is significant damage to open discourse and learning across the country.

"We are a government, a society that purports to protect freedom of speech, the freedom to access information to make up our own minds, to engage in a broadly liberal education," she says. "And we're now finding that we have a movement to shut down that conversation, to deny those rights, particularly to young people."

'COVID Lemonade'

According to Tiffany Justice, co-founder of the parents group Moms for Liberty, the surge in parental interest can be attributed, at least in part, to the remote learning policies schools implemented during the Covid-19 pandemic. For the first time, they say, many parents had an up-close view of what their children were being taught—

and they didn't like it. She calls it "Covid lemonade," because the pandemic had a silver lining.

"We had never really been able to get parents as invigorated as they have been seeing the curriculum up close and personal while they were sitting with their child doing the work," she says. "We saw it as an opportunity to really engage parents even more and to get them involved in their children's education."

Social media has also proved to have a potent effect on the scope of the movement. Activists says it has helped their groups organise across the U.S., as parents learn that they are not alone in their concern. On the other side, groups like the American Library Association have found the same books identified in complaints turn up again and again, as lists—like the one on the No Left Turn websites - are circulated online.

"Social media is amplifying and driving both the messages of these groups that are pursuing a particular agenda, as well as individual challenges that crop up in a community," Caldwell-Stone says.

At the heart of the issue is a debate over the role of parents, schools and the rights of students in the classroom. Both Levin-Sheldon and Justice point out that until children turn 18 they are minors, and parents should be able to review the ideas and subject matters to which their children are exposed—even if that's not supervision all parents want to exercise at home or in the classroom.

Free-speech proponents counter that libraries are meant to serve an entire community of students, not just the ones with the most prudish parents. And although students are not adults, they still have rights—and agency. A dialogue between parents, teachers and librarians is important, but if teenagers seek out information on a topic of interest, they should have access to it.

"There's this notion that young people are in search of the most illicit material in every area of their lives, all the time," says Jonathan Friedman, director of Free Expression and Education at PEN America, an author's free-speech group. "I don't think that's true. I think people go to a library there's usually an alignment between reader and text."

The Politics of Anger

As the push to pass judgement on—and remove—certain books from schools has become a national drive with national attention from conservative and liberal media, tempers have become increasingly frayed.

A school board meeting in Flagler County, Florida, to discuss the removal of the book *All Boys Aren't Blue* devolved into obscenity-laced protests and counter-protests. (The board's decision to approve the book's use was ultimately overruled by a county official).

Meetings in other parts of the U.S. have had to be cancelled or delayed because of threats against public officials. During a school board meeting in Carmel, Indiana, last July, where parents were taking turns reading out explicit passages from books that they believed should be removed from their school library, a man was arrested after a handgun fell out of his pocket.

Levin-Sheldon is quick to note that her group does not approve of such parental conduct and they seek to train their members to behave "respectfully and professional" at school board meetings. Justice agrees, calling her members "joyful warriors," but adds that parents have reason to be angry.

"Yeah, they're upset," she says. "Their kids aren't learning in school. They're sending their kids to school and their kids are learning more about—who knows? Not reading and writing."

Anger can be a potent force in politics, and conservative politicians—and Republican-dominated legislatures—have sought to harness the passion.

Last November, Republican Glenn Youngkin won the Virginia governorship by campaigning on education and parental rights. One of his television adverts featured a mother who objected to Morrison's *Beloved* being taught in her son's high-school English class.

As November's mid-term elections approach, with control of the U.S. Congress and many state governments at stake, more candidates on the right are following suit.

Matt Krause, the Texas legislator with the 850-book list, is running for state attorney general. On Tuesday, the Indiana state Senate approved a bill that would allow the criminal prosecution of school librarians for disseminating "material harmful to minors." The Oklahoma legislature is considering a bill that would ban public school libraries from offering any books on sexuality or gender identity.

Friedman warns that efforts to remove books will have an adverse impact on librarians and school officials, who could engage in "soft censorship" by pre-emptively pulling titles they worry could spark controversy. It could also have a chilling effect on authors and publishers, who might shy away from controversial topics and stifle their creativity.

"If you are telling a story that's on the borderline of any of these issues right now, you're going to think twice about writing in a way that might get banned or draw national attention," he says. "You're not going to publish that book; you're not going to give that talk publicly about it."

Ashley Hope Perez is one of those authors feeling the pressure. In a recent issue of *Texas Monthly*, she describes how she was harassed after her book *Out of Darkness* was criticised as being obscene in meeting of a school board near Austin.

"Ugly phone messages calling me a 'degenerate piece of -', emails that were little more than expletives strung together, social media comments saying I was 'literally SATAN' and suggestions that I hang myself," she writes. "The attacks on *Out of Darkness* say far more about our cultural moment than they do about my book."

She notes that her book was first published six years ago with little controversy. The political ground, it seems, has shifted significantly since then.

Viewpoint 2

> *"Though there has been a significant uptick in book censorship attempts, the arguments to ban books are as old as books themselves. They are also as flimsy as a century-old dime novel."*

Book Bans Are Fundamentally Wrong

Jay Pfeifer

In this viewpoint, Jay Pfeifer looks at the long, complicated history of book bans and argues that the underlying premise of those bans is wrong on a fundamental level. Talking to a professor who frequently teaches a course in which students study specific cases of book controversies, Pfeifer observes that many book-banning arguments are driven by the idea that books should represent an ideal world and that depictions of non-ideal worlds reflect an endorsement of that idea. This logic has been behind arguments for limiting students from reading everything from The Catcher in the Rye *to the* Captain Underpants *series. Jay Pfeifer works as the director of media relations at Davidson College, a private liberal arts college in North Carolina.*

As you read, consider the following questions:

1. According to this viewpoint, should books show the world as we would like it to be or the way we believe it is?

"Book Bans on the Rise, and Consistently Counterproductive, Prof Says," by Jay Pfeifer, Davidson College, February 16, 2022.

2. Why does this viewpoint argue that limiting books in schools is counterproductive?
3. Why would a book series like *Captain Underpants* get challenged in schools?

As school board meetings erupt into shouting matches, an increasing number of states and school districts are moving to ban books. A North Carolina school board decided that *Dear Martin*, a young adult novel about a Black high school student who is racially profiled, could no longer be an assigned 10th grade text after one parent complained about language and sexual references. Similarly, a Tennessee school board voted unanimously to ban *Maus*, the Pulitzer prize-winning graphic novel about one family's Holocaust experience, from the eighth grade classroom because of eight curse words and one panel depicting a nude woman.

A recent report compiled by PEN America, a non-profit that supports freedom of expression in literature, points to a "rapid acceleration" of book censorship in U.S. schools. Over the past school year, 1,648 titles were banned by districts in 32 states.

Though there has been a significant uptick in book censorship attempts, the arguments to ban books are as old as books themselves. They are also as flimsy as a century-old dime novel.

Shireen Campbell, professor of English, director of the Writing Center and acting chair of Educational Studies, frequently teaches a course in which students study specific cases of book controversies.

"One question is at the root of all these arguments: Should books show the world as we would like it to be or the way we believe it is?" Campbell said. "Many book-banning arguments are driven by the idea that books should represent an ideal world. Of course, that "ideal" often excludes large numbers of people or ignores conflicting points of view."

According to her, most attempts to ban books or censor material are not only unsuccessful but also genuinely counterproductive.

Banned books frequently become more popular due to the negative attention. The "Streisand Effect" played out just a few weeks ago as *Maus* shot to the top of Amazon's best-seller list in response to the McMinn County School board decision.

Campbell walked us through three book controversies to illuminate and deconstruct the urge to ban books.

Are Books Endorsements?

First published in 1997, *Captain Underpants* follows the adventures of two fourth-grade class clowns who hypnotize their mean principal. In the process, their comic book character superhero, Captain Underpants, becomes real.

"Full of potty humor, petty adults, and sight gags, children who struggle to read or dislike reading frequently credit these books with bringing them into improved literacy and a reading habit."

Popularity brings controversy. The series received the top ranking in 2012 and 2013 on the challenges list by ALA Office for Intellectual Freedom for reasons including offensive language, unsuited for age group, and violence.

According to Campbell, these *Captain Underpants* objections reflect two assumptions:

- Books should show an "ideal" world.
- Books that show less than "ideal" behavior or attitudes, such as children who eat junk food, lie, or make fun of adults, endorse what they show and will encourage readers to embrace that content.

"People conflate what is in a book with the idea that the actions are being endorsed," Campbell said. "We read literature in which people behave in problematic ways all the time. Showing something doesn't mean endorsing it. When people read *Macbeth*, or see the play, we understand why Macbeth murders, but we also understand that he deteriorates morally in a quest for power."

Can Books Violate Student Conduct Codes?

The 1951 classic *The Catcher in the Rye* tracks a couple of tumultuous days in the life of Holden, a rich, troubled kid who has flunked repeatedly out of prep schools and who sees the adult world as full of "phonies" and hypocrites. The first-person narrator is a deeply troubled, idealistic kid; it is clear to any reader that Holden is lost, endangered and mentally unstable.

This novel, like many on Radcliffe's Top 100 Books of the 20th century, has been widely acclaimed and often attacked. In Glynn County, Georgia, in 2001, a school board member objected to *Catcher in the Rye* because profanity in the novel contradicted the school district's character education program.

"This argument leads down a road where huge numbers of books would be banned," Campbell said. "The decision to get books with 'bad words' out of schools snowballed until the district realized that if they purged every such book, they would have to remove multiple classics, including the works of Shakespeare."

Do Books Really Influence Behavior?

Marjane Satrapi's *Persepolis* recounts her experiences growing up in 1970s and 1980s Iran, through the Islamic Revolution and the war with Iraq. The book has been translated into more than 40 languages and received multiple awards. Satrapi spoke at Davidson in 2014 to a sell-out crowd in Duke Family Performance Hall.

In March 2013, Chicago Public Schools administrators abruptly pulled the book from some classrooms because of torture scenes. Ultimately the book was approved for use in grade 11 classrooms, removed from grade seven classrooms, and reviewed for use in grade eight through 10 classrooms.

In 2014, objections in Oregon and Texas as well as Illinois continued, with details revealing that some parents didn't want their high school students being assigned a book about Muslims. Reading about the "other," whether of a different religion, race, ethnicity, or point of view, it seems, is dangerous because it might make readers more understanding of that other.

What Is the Impact of Media Violence on Children?

The short answer is, no one really knows. But research shows that viewing (or playing) violent content could increase the chance that a child will act aggressively—especially if other risk factors are present, such as growing up in a violent home.

Heavy exposure to violent media can lead to desensitization too. And parents' choices about their own media intake can affect kids. A study by the Annenberg Public Policy Center at the University of Pennsylvania found that parents who watched a lot of movies were more likely to say it was OK for younger kids to watch movies that had R-rated violence and sexual content.

You won't be able to avoid all exposure to violent media. The entertainment industry is always going to try to capture audiences with extreme imagery that tops whatever came before. But in your own home, you have a lot of control over what your kids watch, see, and play—and research shows that kids whose parents actively manage their media consume less and make quality choices on their own.

It's really easy to find media that's free of violence and that your kids will enjoy. There may be a time when your kid is ready to handle more violent media—and you can introduce it age-appropriately and discuss it as a family. In the meantime, choose movies that aren't too scary, find alternatives to violent video games, and seek out media that helps kids develop empathy.

"What's the impact of media violence on kids?," Common Sense Media, June 4, 2020.

So, Do Books Have the Influence Ascribed to Them?

"Research strongly suggests that behaviors such as teen drinking, smoking and sexual activity are influenced by many factors, ranging from parental behavior and home environment to media inputs (advertising in mass media specifically) and peer influence. Books, however, are not on the list," Campbell said.

"Yet, would-be censors are right to fear the power of a book. Scholarship strongly correlates reading, which allows us to share experiences of fictional characters, to how we understand and project the mental states of people around us. Books do engage readers in the lives of others and suggest other modes of being. In this sense, books can make us more open.

"We can roll our eyes at what seem to be foolish objections and find comfort in knowing how often such complaints fail," Campbell said. "In instances where a ban holds, often communities rally and offer alternate conversations, such as the free course Davidson Professor Scott Denham has subsequently designed and is offering to any eighth grader or high school student in McGinn County, where the book was banned."

But even when book complaints in a specific school or community lead to naught, and they often do, the ultimate impact is negative, Campbell said.

Will new teachers stick to curriculum with "tried and true" books rather than try new content? Do libraries on fixed budgets replace materials that disappear when patrons deliberately take and lose content they find objectionable?

Viewpoint 3

> *"Descriptions of characters' physical appearances have been changed, including the removal of words such as 'fat,' 'ugly' and 'black.'"*

Censoring Offensive Language Doesn't Benefit Students

Jessie Tu

This viewpoint by Jessie Tu takes a look at a recent controversy surrounding a move by the estate of the late British author Roald Dahl to edit some of the language used in the UK editions of his books. These changes came about upon the recommendation of sensitivity readers the estate hired to examine the texts around the same time that the estate was negotiating a sale of its intellectual property to the popular streaming company Netflix. Tu makes the argument that these efforts are ultimately futile, since correcting children's books won't do anything to stop children from enacting or perpetrating racist or discriminatory behavior and only poses bigger questions about the classic texts that are left unchanged. Tu is a writer at the website Women's Agenda and the author of the novel A Lonely Girl is a Dangerous Thing, *which was published in 2020.*

"Progressive or futile? 'Offensive' words removed from Roald Dahl classics," by Jessie Tu, Women's Agenda, February 20, 2023.

As you read, consider the following questions:

1. What are some of the official reasons that have been given for changing the language in Roald Dahl's books?
2. According to this viewpoint, how did the public react to these changes?
3. In what way is changing the language in a book both different from and similar to "banning" it?

Roald Dahl's books have been edited and rewritten to erase language deemed offensive in today's social English vernacular.

The publisher of Dahl's works, including *Matilda, Charlie and the Chocolate Factory, James and the Giant Peach,* and *The Witches* announced over the weekend that they have hired sensitivity readers to remove some words and rewrite some text in the UK editions to ensure the books "can continue to be enjoyed by all today."

So What Are the Changes?

Descriptions of characters' physical appearances have been changed, including the removal of words such as "fat", "ugly" and "black."

The Telegraph compared new editions of Dahl's books to past editions, and found that in *The Twits*, Mrs Twit is no longer "ugly and beastly" but simply, "beastly."

In *James and the Giant Peach,* originally published in 1961, the Centipede chants: "Aunt Sponge was terrifically fat / And tremendously flabby at that," and, "Aunt Spiker was thin as a wire / And dry as a bone, only drier."

These lines have now been removed and replaced with: "Aunt Sponge was a nasty old brute / And deserved to be squashed by the fruit," and, "Aunt Spiker was much of the same / And deserves half of the blame."

Subtler changes have also been made, such as the removal of the word "fat" in the lines: "The fat shopkeeper shouted" has become "the shopkeeper shouted," and "the fat shopkeeper said" has become "the shopkeeper said."

Gendered terms have also been neutralised, such as the term "Cloud-*Men*", which has become "Cloud-*People*." References to "boys and girls" have been changed to "children," while "mothers and fathers," has been changed to "parents."

The term "female" has also been altered.

In *Matilda*, published in 1988, Miss Trunchbull was originally described as "most formidable female." She is now described as a "most formidable woman."

Her "great horsey face" has been changed to "face," and "eight nutty little idiots" has become "eight nutty little boys."

In *Charlie and the Chocolate Factory*, published in 1964, an original line read: "The man behind the counter looked fat and well-fed. He had big lips and fat cheeks and a very fat neck."

The new editions have entirely erased these lines. Other lines that describe fatness, including "The fat around his neck bulged out all around the top of his collar like a rubber ring"; "Who's the big fat boy?"; and "Enormous, isn't he?" have all been removed, though Augustus Gloop is now described as "enormous" instead of "fat." Oompa Loompas, previously described as "small men", are now "small people."

In *The Witches*, first published in 1983, an additional sentence has been added to a description about the witches and their wigs: "There are plenty of other reasons why women might wear wigs and there is certainly nothing wrong with that."

"Fat little brown mouse" has been changed to "little brown mouse" and a line regarding a boy needing to "go on a diet" has been removed.

Official Reasons

Puffin and the Roald Dahl Story Company, which owns the books, made the changes in conjunction with Inclusive Minds, an organisation founded ten years ago that aims to promote equality, diversity, inclusion and accessibility in children's books.

Alexandra Strick, a co-founder of Inclusive Minds, told *The Guardian* they "aim to ensure authentic representation, by working closely with the book world and with those who have lived experience of any facet of diversity."

The Roald Dahl Story Co. which was acquired by Netflix in September 2021, released a statement, saying they seek to "ensure that Roald Dahl's wonderful stories and characters continue to be enjoyed by all children today."

"When publishing new print runs of books written years ago, it's not unusual to review the language used alongside updating other details including a book's cover and page layout," the statement read.

"Our guiding principle throughout has been to maintain the storylines, characters, and the irreverence and sharp-edged spirit of the original text. Any changes made have been small and carefully considered."

The *LA Times* cited an email from Roald Dahl Story Co. spokesman Rick Behari where he explained, "the overall changes are small both in terms of actual edits which have been made and also in terms of the overall percentage of texts which has been changed."

"As part of our process to review the language used we worked in partnership with Inclusive Minds, a collective for people who are passionate about inclusion and accessibility in children's literature," the spokesman added.

"The current review began in 2020, before Dahl was acquired by Netflix. It was led by Puffin and Roald Dahl Story Company together."

The latest editions of the books include the clause: "The wonderful words of Roald Dahl can transport you to different worlds and introduce you to the most marvellous characters. This book was written many years ago, and so we regularly review the language to ensure that it can continue to be enjoyed by all today."

Public Reaction

The announcement of these latest changes to Dahl's books met a wave of public backlash from prominent literary figures, including Salman Rushdie, who tweeted:

"Roald Dahl was no angel but this is absurd censorship. Puffin Books and the Dahl estate should be ashamed."

Many critics are calling the changes "woke," "pointless" and "dangerous."

The Telegraph's arts and entertainment editor Anita Singh said "The thing that annoys me about the Roald Dahl changes is how stupid they are."

"A ban on the word 'fat' yet keeping in the rest of the description in which Augustus Gloop is clearly fat."

Translator and writer, Anton Hur, said on Twitter: "This has less to do with censorship and more to do with an estate cynically squeezing out every last bit of money they can from the IP of a long-dead person. Not all books deserve be passed on, not every author's work is a classic. We can let some of it go. It's ok."

CEO of PEN America, Suzanne Nossel, tweeted a long thread, expressing her alarm at the "hundreds of changes" to venerated works by @roald_dahlin a purported effort to scrub the books of that which might offend someone."

"Amidst fierce battles against book bans and strictures on what can be taught and read, selective editing to make works of literature conform to particular sensibilities could represent a dangerous new weapon," she wrote.

"Those who might cheer specific edits to Dahl's work should consider how the power to rewrite books might be used in the hands of those who do not share their values and sensibilities. We understand the impulse to want to ensure that great works of children's literature do not alienate kids or foster stereotypes."

Nossel describes the "regrettable outcome" of having "beloved works" including Dr. Seuss books withdrawn entirely out of concern for causing offence.

"The problem with taking license to re-edit classic works is that there is no limiting principle," she continues. "You start out wanting to replace a word here and a word there, and end up inserting entirely new ideas (as has been done to Dahl's work).

"Literature is meant to be surprising and provocative. That's part of its potency. By setting out to remove any reference that might cause offence you dilute the power of storytelling."

Nossel believes a better solution can be made by offering introductory context that "...prepares people for what they are about to read, and helps them understand the setting in which it was written."

"If an editor, publisher or estate believes they must go beyond that, readers should be put on notice about what changes have been made and those wishing to read the work in its original form should have that opportunity."

"Changes should be kept as surgical as possible with expert input to uphold the integrity and authenticity of the original work. So much of literature could be construed as offensive to someone—based on race, gender, religion, age, socio-economic status or myriad other factors. Such portrayals are vital topics for discussion and debate, leading to new insights."

Deputy literary editor of London's *Sunday Times*, Laura Hackett agrees, saying the editors at Puffin "...should be ashamed of the botched surgery they've carried out on some of the finest children's literature in Britain."

"As for me, I'll be carefully stowing away my old, original copies of Dahl's stories, so that one day my children can enjoy them in their full, nasty, colorful glory," she tweeted.

Dahl's Complicated Legacy

Since his death in 1990, Dahl has been criticised for his history of alleged anti-Semitic remarks made during his lifetime.

In December 2020, Dahl's family released a statement, apologising for the "hurt" his books caused.

"The Dahl family and the Roald Dahl Story Company deeply apologise for the lasting and understandable hurt caused by some of Roald Dahl's statements," the statement read.

"Those prejudiced remarks are incomprehensible to us and stand in marked contrast to the man we knew and to the values at the heart of Roald Dahl's stories, which have positively impacted young people for generations. We hope that, just as he did at his best, at his absolute worst, Roald Dahl can help remind us of the lasting impact of words."

Progressive or Futile?

Charlie and the Chocolate Factory was first published in 1964—a very different time. Back then, Dahl could describe Oompa-Loompas as African Pygmy people whom Wonka had "smuggled" out of Africa in crates to work in his factory—and for that description to not cause any offence to mainstream audiences.

We're sympathetic to the publisher's intentions. We understand the supposed pursuit in wanting to correct the wrongs of the past—but correcting wrongs in a few texts doesn't systemically correct anything in the long run, does it? And if you're going to rewrite history (there's a supposed timelessness about Dahl's books that can explain why he's still being so widely read today) then what should we do about 'offensive' movies from fifty years ago? One hundred years ago? Why isn't the over-famed and extremely problematic "Birth of a Nation" completely destroyed?

What about other 'classic' books, like *To Kill A Mockingbird*, which is problematic for a whole other host of reasons?

Correcting children's books won't stop children from enacting or perpetrating racist or discriminatory behaviour. If we censor words like this from old texts then we bar ourselves from having important conversations about language, and hinder our ability to explain to future generations why we wouldn't use words like that today.

We agree with Suzanne Nossell, who concluded her tweets by saying: "If we start down the path of trying to correct for perceived slights instead of allowing readers to receive and react to books as written, we risk distorting the work of great authors and clouding the essential lens that literature offers on society."

Viewpoint 4

> *"Banning books has been going on for centuries—and it's not unique to the United States, either."*

Book Banning Happens Around the World

John Maher and Ed Nawotka

In this viewpoint, John Maher and Ed Nawotka consider some of the books that have been banned and challenged, largely by governments, around the world in countries as disparate as Brazil and Bangladesh. The reasons given for the bans often vary. For instance, a book that won a major award in France would ultimately become banned—complete with bookstore owners sentenced to prison—over allegations that it contained information "distributing military secrets." Another example is a book that explains how to escape Cuba by boat, which became banned in Cuba. Other cultural anxieties are more familiar, however; a Marvel comic book that depicted its two protagonists kissing landed the ire of the mayor of Rio de Janiero, who warned that the book was trying to "spread homosexuality to children." John Maher and Ed Nawotka both write for Publishers Weekly, *a trade magazine that covers the publishing world.*

As you read, consider the following questions:

1. What are some of different reasons that are often given for banning books in countries like Cuba or Egypt?

"Where Are Books Banned? All Across the Globe," by John Maher and Ed Nawotka, Publishers Weekly, September 27, 2019. Reprinted by permission.

2. Are some of the reasons similar to the ones used in book challenges in the U.S.?
3. Do book challenges reflect the nuances of local culture? Why or why not?

Banning books has been going on for centuries—and it's not unique to the United States, either. To shed light on worldwide censorship of literature in honor of last week's Banned Books Week, Global English Editing, an online professional editing and proofreading service, put together a map of the world showcasing book censorship in some of the planet's most prominent nations.

"Opposition to specific literature is nothing new, and censorship is nearly as old as writing itself," a Global English Editing representative told *PW*. "Official censorship and the origins of the word *censor* can be traced back to the office of censor, established in Rome in 443 BCE. Here, and in other ancient societies such as China, it was considered a virtuous means to control and mold the character of the people. However, if you think the banning of books was restricted to bygone eras less civilized than today, think again."

In response to the map, a number of publishers worldwide provided *PW* with a list of additional banned titles, spotlighting censorship worldwide.

Bangladesh: *Naree* by Humayun Azad

This Bengali feminist treatise on the role of women and their struggle for equal rights in civilizations run by men criticizes revered figures such as Rabindranath Tagore, among others. "The book was banned for five years after it was published in 1994, but then, after a court order, was released for publication five years later," says Mitia Osman, publisher of Agamee Prakashani.

Brazil: *Avengers: The Children's Crusade* by Allan Heinberg, illus. by Jim Cheung

Earlier this month, the mayor of Rio de Janiero tried to have this Marvel comic book removed from the city's book fair, saying it was "objectionable to minors" because it featured an illustration of two protagonists—the superheroes Hulkling and Wiccan, who are boyfriends—kissing. Earlier, a city counsellor blamed the comic for "spread[ing] homosexuality to children." As a result, booksellers sold out of the comic, and the national newspaper *Folha de Sao Paolo* subsequently put the image of the men kissing on its front page.

Cuba: *Wet Foot Dry Foot* by Pedro Ramirez Gonzalez

The book explains the process of escaping Cuba by boat—and the emotional toll that it takes on the migrants and those left behind. "The reason it is banned is self-explanatory," says Heidi Heinzof the Guantanamera Literary Agency, which represents the author.

Egypt: *The Angel: The Egyptian Spy Who Saved Israel* by Uri Bar-Joseph

In April 2018, Khalid Lutfi, owner of the Tanmia Bookshop and Publisher in Cairo, was arrested and sentenced to prison on charges of "distributing military secrets" related to his plans to publish *The Angel*. Lufti remains imprisoned to this day, and was just this year awarded the Prix Voltaire from the International Publishers Association.

VIEWPOINT 5

> *"The increasing presence of identity politics within the political realm as well as workplaces and schools has also meant a long-awaited battle for inclusion for some, and unnecessary and divisive debates on race and sexuality for others, further fueling ongoing culture wars."*

Book Bans Threaten Democracy

Breanna Crossman

In this viewpoint, Breanna Crossman explains the issue of partisanship in the U.S. and how it relates to identity politics, culture wars, and book bans. She argues that a number of factors have caused the current culture war to worsen, and that schools often serve as the battleground for these conflicts. Crossman also explains that culture wars always precede violent conflicts in countries, so even though the fact that there is a culture war currently raging in the U.S. doesn't necessarily mean there will be partisan violence, it does mean that the chances of this happening have increased. Book bannings and other forms of censorship caused by this conflict have a detrimental effect on the emotional and intellectual development of students and, by extension, the future of democracy. Breanna Crossman studies international affairs and classics at Georgetown University and has served as editor and social media coordinator for Neutral Citizens Journalism.

"Culture Wars, Book-Banning, and Identity Politics: Symptoms of a Crumbling Democracy?," by Breanna Crossman, Neutral Citizen Journalism, September 7, 2022.

As you read, consider the following questions:

1. How does Crossman define a culture war in this viewpoint?
2. What are some of the main issues dividing Americans in the current culture war, according to this viewpoint?
3. According to data cited in this viewpoint, how much did book bans increase in the U.S. between 2020 and 2021?

America today is one of the most divided nations in the world, according to Pew Research Center. Among 17 countries in Europe, Asia, and North America, Americans were "most likely to say their society was split along partisan, racial, and ethnic lines," with the U.S. also being one of five countries in which more than half the public said their fellow citizens can't agree on basic facts.

Where we stand today in terms of political polarization is the culmination of several controversial social movements and debates about Black Lives Matter, affirmative action, parental rights in education, the legitimacy of the 2020 election, the government response to the COVID-19 pandemic, and more. The increasing presence of identity politics within the political realm as well as workplaces and schools has also meant a long-awaited battle for inclusion for some, and unnecessary and divisive debates on race and sexuality for others, further fueling ongoing culture wars. Fears over what is being taught in the classroom, from the Critical Race Theory to gender identity, have inflamed much of the nation in fierce debate, leading many school districts to ban or censor books at a higher rate than any other time in recent history. So how and why has America become a breeding ground for fear, mistrust, and disagreement, and will we be able to reconcile our diverging perspectives before our democracy crumbles?

What Is a Culture War?

The definition of a culture war is fiercely debated and is frequently applied during debates about hot-button social issues including social justice, racism, feminism, and LGBTQ+ rights. It now serves largely as an umbrella term, encapsulating the ongoing clash between American citizens over contemporary issues, primarily taking part on various social media platforms.

Conflicts in America's ongoing culture war have led to violence, political polarization, and the rampant spread of misinformation. To some, the increasingly obvious divide between political parties and growing mistrust in government institutions indicate the crumbling of our democracy.

"Democracy, in my view, is an agreement that we will not kill each other over our differences, but instead we'll talk through those differences. And part of what's troubling is that I'm beginning to see signs of the justification for violence," says James Hunter, an American sociologist credited with inventing the term "Culture Wars." "Culture wars always precede shooting wars. They don't *necessarily* lead to a shooting war, but you never have a shooting war without a culture war prior to it, because culture provides the justifications for violence."

Indeed, Hunter saw the insurrection of January 6th, 2020, where a mob of Donald Trump supporters sieged the Capitol in an attempt to overturn the results of the 2020 election as the first shots in the physical realization of America's culture war. The lingering reluctance to accept the 2020 election results among some conservatives across America indicated a larger epidemic of fear-mongering by politicians and misleading narratives pushed by mainstream media channels.

Culture wars have also reached even the upper echelons of the American judicial system. Supreme Court Justice Ketanji Brown Jackson was asked several questions relating to race and Critical Race Theory during her confirmation, to the ire of many Democrats. Tennessee Senator Marsha Blackburn falsely claimed that Jackson would utilize CRT as an important resource when making decisions on the Supreme Court. Jackson was later confirmed as the first black woman on the United States Supreme Court by the Senate, despite opposition by many Republicans. The tumultuous confirmation of Supreme Court Justice Amy Coney Barett, nominated by former President Donald Trump, also included many probes into her conservative religious background that some felt would influence her decisions on the Supreme Court.

Supreme Court Justice Clarence Thomas has critiqued the highly politicized criticisms of the Supreme Court Justices, largely blaming cancel culture as the culprit. "You can cavalierly talk about packing or stacking the court. You can cavalierly talk about doing this or doing that. At some point the institution is going to be compromised," he stated. "By doing this, you continue to chip away at the respect of the institutions that the next generation is going to need if they're going to have civil society," A few months after these remarks, the Court's decision to overturn *Roe v. Wade*, a landmark 1973 ruling that gave American women the right to abortion, led to nationwide protest and further scrutiny of the Supreme Court Justices.

Higher education is also a battleground for culture wars, especially revolving around identity politics. College campuses have also become fraught with debate over affirmative action and equity, with some decrying affirmative action itself as racist, with others saying affirmative action prevents racism. A brief submitted by the anti-affirmative action group Students for Fair Admissions sued Harvard and the University of North Carolina over affirmative action within their college admissions processes. The brief, which is now being reviewed by the Supreme Court, argued that Harvard discriminates against Asian-American applicants and gives unfair advantages to black and Latino applicants.

Harvard released a brief rejecting this assertion, stating "Nothing in the text of history of the Fourteenth Amendment suggests that universities must uniquely exclude race from the multitude of factors considered in assembling a class of students best able to learn from each other." The brief also stated that

Harvard's admission process complies with past Court rulings that permit the consideration of race in college admissions.

UNC submitted a brief with similar arguments, and lower courts ruled in favor of both colleges. However, many believe that the newly Conservative-dominated Supreme Court may reconsider these rulings. Some fear that if affirmative action is scrapped, enrollment of minority students will drop significantly, reducing diversity on college campuses. Others, however, believe that college admissions should be race-blind, only determined by a student's academic or athletic merit.

Meanwhile, other states including California have already voted to end race consideration in college admissions. A ban passed in 1996 prevented colleges from including race in considered factors for admissions, leading to the percentages of black and Latino students at prestigious colleges like UCLA plummeting. In 2006, the freshmen class of 5,000 students contained just 96 African-Americans. Since then, UCLA has taken minor steps by using a "holistic review" of applicants, which considers racial background as a factor. Newly proposed legislation called Proposition 16 would also strike the ban on race-conscious college admissions if instituted, ending the state's 24-year ban on affirmative action.

"I think the holistic review process that considers race and ethnicity is a small step toward addressing the problem of underrepresentation of historically disadvantaged groups. I don't think it's enough, but it's better than not having race and ethnicity considered at all." said UCLA Asian American Studies Center director Karen Umemoto. Still, affirmative action remains highly controversial as critics fear it overemphasizes race in the analysis of an applicant and pits minority applicants against each other.

Others have noticed the infiltration of cancel culture into college campuses. Gordon Klein, a professor at UCLA's Andersen School of Management was fired after refusing to give African-American students higher grades in the wake of George Floyd's murder. Klein received death threats for months following this refusal. In 2016, in a highly-publicized controversy at Yale University, professor

Nicholas Christakis resigned after an email about culturally insensitive Halloween costumes went viral. The email, written by his wife Erika, included a segment where Christakis suggested students "look away, or tell them you are offended" if they come across a racist costume. Christakis's resignation signaled a move in the right direction for accountability and inclusion on college campuses for some, an assault on free speech for others.

How Did We Get Here?

While political partisanship and disagreement have always been a major part of any democracy, tensions between parties rose to a new extreme under the presidency of Donald Trump. Trump, a former businessman known for his controversial and startling comments regarding women and immigrants. Prior to the tumultuous 2020 election, 80% of registered Democrats and Republicans stated that their differences with the other side were about core American values, while roughly 90% stated that a victory by the opposing party would cause "lasting harm" to the United States, according to Pew Research Center.

This division during the COVID-19 pandemic caused the deaths of 6.44 million people worldwide. Ant-vax conspiracies spread rapidly online, causing some to doubt the effectiveness and purpose of COVID-19 vaccines. School lockdowns and virtual learning sparked outrage as some felt children were being denied quality education and forced to wear masks. Yet, Americans regarded the government's handling of the pandemic in dramatically different ways. According to Pew Research Center, 76% of Republicans felt the U.S. had done a good job dealing with the COVID-19 pandemic, compared to 29% of people who did not identify with the Republican party. This widely divergent viewpoint led many to believe that the U.S. had reached the zenith of political polarization as Americans fundamentally disagreed on how to manage public health disasters. 77% of Americans believed the country was more divided after the pandemic than before, according to Pew Research Center.

Americans were also deeply divided over racial justice movements in the wake of George Floyd's murder in May of 2020. When a video of policeman Derek Chauvin kneeling on Floyd's neck for over 9 minutes was widely circulated on social media, protests broke out across the country. In some major cities, protests led to property destruction and physical conflicts between protesters and police. In Minneapolis, a police precinct was set on fire, while police tear-gassed protests in Tulsa, Oklahoma, and Madison, Wisconsin. The National Guard was activated in 28 states to stop violent looting and arson. In some locations, peaceful protesters exercising their constitutional right to protest were beaten and fired upon by officers.

A few months after the murder, policeman Derek Chauvin was sentenced to 21 years in federal prison, while his three colleagues who were present during the murder were also tried and convicted on charges of manslaughter. The Black Lives Matter movement that increased media scrutiny of police nationwide was countered by the All Lives Matter Movement, which deemed the motto "black lives matter" as divisive. The All Lives Matter movement was supported by several high-profile politicians, including former President Donald Trump, former Vice President Mike Pence, and prominent conservatives including Rudy Giuliani. While the impacts of the Black Lives Matter and the All Lives Matter movements are yet to be fully realized, both social movements signify the wider racial reckoning and culture wars Americans are experiencing.

Book-Bannings and Censorship Plague Schools, Libraries

In another branch of the ongoing culture war, libraries across the nation are now facing unprecedented book bannings. According to the American Library Association, in 2021 there were 729 book challenges attempting to ban 1,579 books, which is double the amount in 2020. The titles being targeted mainly involved sensitive topics including racism, LGBTQ+ identities, and gender.

In 2021, the ten most challenged books were "Gender Queer" by Maia Kobabe, "Lawn Boy" by Jonathan Evison, "All Boys Aren't Blue" by George M. Johnson, "Out of Darkness" by Ashley Perez, "The Hate U Give" by Angie Thomas, "The Absolutely True Diary of a Part-Time Indian" by Sherman Alexie, "Me and Earl and the Dying Girl" by Jesse Andrews, "The Bluest Eye" by Toni Morrison, "This Book is Gay" by Juno Dawson, and "Beyond Magenta" by Susan Kuklin. Other historically banned classics that have been re-censored include "To Kill a Mockingbird" by Harper Lee, "The Color Purple" by Alice Walker, and "1984" by George Orwell.

In Tennessee, Art Spiegelman's Pulitzer Prize-winning graphic memoir "Maus" was voted unanimously to be removed from the McMinn County School Board to be removed from the school curriculum. Elected representatives have also had an increasing role in book banning. South Carolina governor Henry McMaster and Florida governor Ron DeSantis both criticized the book "Gender Queer," with McMaster calling the book's content on sexuality "obscene." In an effort to increase transparency, DeSantis signed a bill into law that required schools to make all assigned books available for parental review.

For some, the inclusion of supposedly age-inappropriate books for children must be countered by increased parental involvement in education. Groups including Moms for Liberty have taken action to increase the voice of parents in school curriculums to counter books that contain sexual or violent content. Moms for Liberty is a Florida-based parents' rights group that was born out of parents' anxieties over the "indoctrination" of children in schools across America. The grassroots organization has grown to 200 chapters with 100,000 members in 40 states, all working towards giving parents a voice in their children's education. Much of their efforts today are to work with elected officials to supervise what types of books can be read in schools and libraries. Moms for Liberty has been recognized by several high-profile officials, including Ron DeSantis, who lauded their efforts to work with school PTA's to review books before they reach the classroom. DeSantis was also widely criticized and celebrated for signing a law into effect that banned discussion about gender identity and sexual identity in kindergarten through third grade, dubbed the "Don't Say Gay" bill by progressives.

The Moms for Liberty chapter in Kitsap County, Washington recently criticized the frequently-banned book "Gender Queer," with Chapter chair Joy Gjservold calling the book "pornographic." She criticized the high school teacher who taught passages of the book to students "with no warning to parents."

"There was no consideration given that parents' religious beliefs might say they don't want them reading things like that. We're not trying to ban books. We're just trying to have it age-appropriate." Gjersvold said.

Book banning and censorship movements have been widely condemned by librarians, activists, and politicians. "By attacking these books, by attacking the authors, by attacking the subject matter, what they are doing is removing the possibility for conversation," said author Laurie Halse Anderson, whose novel "Speak" has been widely banned for its depiction of sexual assault. Without access to books that deal with sensitive issues, real conversation cannot take place. "You are laying the groundwork for increasing bullying, disrespect, violence, and attacks."

Some worry that librarians and educators will be unfairly penalized for their curriculums due to increased scrutiny of the books read in schools. "The politicization of the topic is what's different than what I've seen in the past," said the chief executive of content at Follett School Solutions, Britten Follett. "It's being driven by legislation, it's being driven by politicians aligning with one side or the other. And in the end, the librarian, teacher or educator is getting caught in the middle."

What Is Next?

In his first speech as president-elect, Joe Biden promised to defend America's democracy and address many of the social issues that have embroiled America in a culture war.

"America is rising anew. Choosing hope over fear. Truth over lies. Light over darkness. After 100 days of rescue and renewal, America is ready for take-off. We are working again. Dreaming again. Discovering again. Leading the world again." President Joe Biden said, before outlining his plans for police accountability, COVID-19 relief bills, and restoring faith in the government. He called on politicians to stop making teachers "targets of culture wars."

Despite these promises, it is unclear what direction America will turn toward with increasingly contentious debates about new issues including the war in Ukraine, U.S.-China relations, and the investigation of former President Trump's actions in office. Whether the culture war will end in further conflict or reconciliation is yet to be seen.

Periodical and Internet Sources Bibliography

The following articles have been selected to supplement the diverse views presented in this chapter.

Terry Aguayo, "Miami-Dade School Board Bans Cuba Book," *New York Times*, June 16, 2006. www.nytimes.com/2006/06/16/education/16cuba.html.

Mic Anderson, "11 Banned Books Through Time," *Britannica*, April 26, 2023. www.britannica.com/story/7-banned-books-through-time.

Elizabeth Blair, "Adults have a lot to say about book bans — but what about kids?," NPR, October 4, 2023. www.npr.org/2023/10/04/1203277224/kids-on-book-bans-during-banned-books-week.

Libby Brooks, "'Out of touch': children's authors describe increasing censorship of books on diversity," the *Guardian*, March 31, 2022. www.theguardian.com/books/2022/mar/31/childrens-authors-describe-worrying-trend-of-censorship-of-books-on-diversity.

Arvyn Cerézo, "What Book Censorship Looks Like Outside the United States," Book Riot, February 8, 2022. bookriot.com/book-censorship-around-the-world.

Nadine Farid Johnson, "The US is inspiring education censorship elsewhere," *Al Jazeera*, January 4, 2023. https://www.aljazeera.com/opinions/2023/1/4/the-us-is-exporting-education-censorship-2.

Jessica Grose, "Book Banning Is About the Illusion of Parental Control," *New York Times*, February 9, 2022. www.nytimes.com/2022/02/09/opinion/book-banning-parents.html.

Christian Holub, "Don't worry, Roald Dahl's original texts will still be published after critics call new editions 'absurd censorship,'" *Entertainment Weekly*, February 24, 2023. ew.com/books/roald-dahl-original-texts-available-after-censorship-criticism.

Danica Kirka, "Salman Rushdie decries 'absurd censorship' of Roald Dahl's classic children's books, with words like 'fat' removed," *Fortune*, February 19, 2023. fortune.com/2023/02/19/salman-rushdie-decries-absurd-censorship-of-roald-dahl-classic-childrens-books.

Max McCoy, "One weird trick for backsliding democracy: Read banned books," *Tennessee Lookout*, December 6, 2021/ tennesseelookout.com/2021/12/06/one-weird-trick-for-backsliding-democracy-read-banned-books.

Paul Ringel, "How Banning Books Marginalizes Children," the *Atlantic*, October 1, 2016. www.theatlantic.com/entertainment/archive/2016/10/how-banned-books-marginalize-children/502424.

Kevin Tschierse, "Barack Obama condemns 'profoundly misguided' book bans," *Deutsche Welle*, July 21, 2023. www.dw.com/en/barack-obama-condemns-profoundly-misguided-book-bans/a-66282411.

Matthew Walther, "The Truth About the 'Censorship' of Roald Dahl," *New York Times*, March 3, 2023. www.nytimes.com/2023/03/03/opinion/roald-dahl-books-changes.html.

Luke Winkie, "US conservative parents push for book bans – and unintentionally make reading cool again," the *Guardian*, December 23, 2021. www.theguardian.com/education/2021/dec/23/us-book-bans-conservative-parents-reading.

For Further Discussion

Chapter 1

1. Why do you think early censorship laws like the Comstock Act also applied to works of art and literature?
2. What's the connection between burning witches and banning books, according to the viewpoint from the Council on Foreign Relations?
3. Based on what you've read in the viewpoints in this chapter, why do so many disputes over free speech end up in the courts? Explain your answer.

Chapter 2

1. Based on the viewpoints you've read in this chapter, why do parents pushing for book bans not trust teachers to make those calls?
2. Based on what you have read, do you think book banning is fundamentally illegal or unconstitutional? Why or why not?
3. Is the political Left or Right more interested in limiting books? Explain your answer.

Chapter 3

1. In what ways is limiting what stories are told in a textbook similar to banning books?
2. How are the motivations of people who want characters in books to be more diverse different from those who want books to be banned from schools? How are they similar?
3. In what parts of the country are parents pushing for limiting books in schools? Why do you think this is the case?

Chapter 4

1. Based on what you've read in this chapter, why do books by ethnic minorities, women, or LGBTQIA+ authors seem to intimidate parents who want to limit those books in schools?

2. What could be the impact of limiting diversity in books that can be found in schools?
3. What factors are behind the latest wave of books bans, according to the viewpoints in this chapter?

Organizations to Contact

The editors have compiled the following list of organizations concerned with the issues debated in this book. The descriptions are derived from materials provided by the organizations. All have publications or information available for interested readers. The list was compiled on the date of publication of the present volume; the information provided here may change. Be aware that many organizations take several weeks or longer to respond to inquiries, so allow as much time as possible.

American Booksellers for Free Expression

333 Westchester Ave.
White Plains, NY 10604
(914) 406-7500
email: info@bookweb.org
website: https://bookweb.org/advocacy/free-expression

This trade group opposes restrictions on the freedom of speech, issues statements on significant free expression controversies, participates in legal cases involving First Amendment rights, and provides education about the importance of free expression to booksellers, other members of the book industry, politicians, the press, and the public. In 2015, the group was operationally folded back into the American Booksellers Association.

American Library Association's Office for Intellectual Freedom

225 Michigan Ave, Suite 1300
Chicago, IL 60601
(312) 280-4221
email: oif@ala.org
website: www.ala.org/aboutala/offices/oif

A direct wing of the American Library Association, its Office for Intellectual Freedom tasks itself with educating "librarians and the general public about the nature and importance of intellectual freedom in libraries," per its website. Its parent group runs an annual event called "Banned Books Week," and the office itself provides free consulting services aimed at school librarians and teachers who are concerned with facing new censorship restrictions.

Comic Book Legal Defense Fund

15110 Boones Ferry Road
Suite 220
Lake Oswego, OR 97035
(212) 679-7151
email: info@cbldf.org
website: https://cbldf.org

A non-profit formed in 1986 to support the First Amendment rights of comic books writers, the group has its own spot in the banned books debate; they're a sponsor of events supporting banned books and come to the legal defense of comic book writers challenging such bans. "Comics are uniquely vulnerable to challenges because the medium thrives on the power of static images, and because there is a lingering stigma that comics are low-value speech," the group says on its website, illuminating its concerns.

First Amendment Center

email: freespeechcenter@mtsu.edu
website: https://firstamendment.mtsu.edu

Started by a notable reporter named John Seigenthaler, largely behind a newspaper called the *Tennessean*, the center is now run by Middle Tennessee State University. Among its various reports and advocacy work, the group also regularly puts out a blog post called "Book Report: A compilation of recent news articles on book banning," which collects recent reporting on the state of booking banning in the U.S. and around the world.

Florida Citizens Alliance

PO Box 697
Marco Island, FL 34146
(239) 250-3320
email: admin@goflca.org
website: https://goflca.org

One state that has been at the forefront of book banning efforts in schools has been Florida, which is where groups like the Florida Citizens Alliance argue that "Florida children are being indoctrinated in a public school system that undermines their individual rights and destroys our nation's founding principles and family values," per their website. Like a lot of the other free speech groups, this one also regularly puts out its own reports.

Freedom to Read Foundation

225 N. Michigan Ave., Suite 1300
Chicago, IL 60611
(312) 280-4226
email: ftrf@ala.org
website: www.ftrf.org

An anti-book banning group that is affiliated with the American Library Association, this non-profit focuses on fighting the prospect of book bans in public libraries and has been involved in doing this since 1969. According to the group, it was started in "response to its members' interest in having adequate means to support and defend librarians whose positions are jeopardized because of their resistance to abridgments of the First Amendment."

Moms for Liberty

981 E Eau Gallie Blvd E
Box 13123
Melbourne, FL 32937
(321) 345-1671
email: info@momsforliberty.org
website: https://momsforliberty.org

Started in 2021, Moms for Liberty has been among the more prominent groups supporting limits on what kinds of books and educational materials children in schools are able to read. Run through a network of chapters throughout the U.S., members of the group have largely opposed contemporary books written by Black people and LGBTQIA+ people, as well as textbooks that depicted instances of police brutality, among other issues.

National Coalition Against Censorship

19 Fulton Street
Suite 407
New York, NY 10038
phone: (212) 807-6222
email: ncac@ncac.org
website: https://ncac.org

Founded in 1974, the National Coalition Against Censorship brings together at least 50 non-profit organizations in the U.S., organizing them around ideas like defending freedom of expression from censorship as well as threats of censorship. The organization aims to fight censorship through education, outreach, and direct advocacy. The group came together in response to a 1973 Supreme Court case called *Miller v. California,* which created new legal language to define ideas like obscenity.

PEN America

588 Broadway #303
New York, NY 10012
(212) 334-1660
email: info@pen.org
website: https://pen.org

One of the most prominent free speech groups out there, PEN America is an organized group representing approximately 7,500 novelists, journalists, nonfiction writers, editors, poets, essayists, playwrights, publishers, translators, agents, and other writing professionals who advocate for freedom in publishing and writing. The group regularly tracks and publishes reports on the state of book bans in the U.S. and elsewhere, noting most recently that "the 2022-23 school year has been marked to date by an escalation of book bans and censorship in classrooms and school libraries across the United States," per their website.

Unite Against Book Bans

225 Michigan Ave, Suite 1300
Chicago, IL 60601
(312) 280-4221
email: shines@alawash.org
website: https://uniteagainstbookbans.org

Another anti-book banning group that's being funded by the American Library Association, this organization started in 2021 in response to the more recent efforts to ban books in schools and elsewhere. According to a press release, they started the organization in order to galvanize "community members to support libraries and respond to the surge in book challenges and other efforts to suppress access to information."

Utah Parents United

email: contact@utahparentsunited.org
website: www.utahparentsunited.org

Based in Farmington, Utah, this group has been described in the press as "a conservative Christian group that pushes for book bans [and] has training videos to help parents pressure teachers." According to its website, the group is run solely by unpaid parent volunteers.

Bibliography of Books

Sharyl Attkisson. *Slanted: How the News Media Taught Us to Love Censorship and Hate Journalism*. New York, NY: Harper, 2020.

Eric Berkowitz. *Dangerous Ideas: A Brief History of Censorship in the West, from the Ancients to Fake News*. Boston, MA: Beacon Press, 2021.

Andrew Doyle. *Free Speech and Why It Matters Why It Matters*. London, UK: Constable & Robinson Limited, 2022.

Barry Glassner. *The Culture of Fear: Why Americans Are Afraid of the Wrong Things*. New York, NY: Basic Books, 2018.

James Griffiths. *The Great Firewall of China: How to Build and Control an Alternative Version of the Internet*. London, UK: Zed Books, 2021.

Claudia Johnson. *Stifled Laughter: One Woman's Story About Fighting Censorship*. Wheat Ridge, CO: Fulcrum Publishing, 2023.

Emily Knox. *Book Banning in 21st-Century America*. Lanham, MD: Rowman & Littlefield Publishers, 2015.

James LaRue. *On Censorship: A Public Librarian Examines Cancel Culture in the US*. Wheat Ridge, CO: Fulcrum Publishing, 2023.

Kristin Pekoll. *Beyond Banned Books: Defending Intellectual Freedom Throughout Your Library*. Chicago, IL: ALA Editions, 2021.

H. L. Pohlman. *Free Speech and Censorship: Examining the Facts*. Santa Barbara, CA: ABC-CLIO, 2019.

Margaret E. Roberts. *Censored: Distraction and Diversion Inside China's Great Firewall*. Princeton, NJ: Princeton University Press, 2020.

Pat R. Scales. *Books Under Fire: A Hit List of Banned and Challenged Children's Books*. Chicago, IL: ALA Editions, 2021.

Nadine Strossen. *HATE: Why We Should Resist It with Free Speech, Not Censorship.* Oxford, UK: Oxford University Press, 2018.

Amy Werbel. *Lust on Trial: Censorship and the Rise of American Obscenity in the Age of Anthony Comstock*. New York, NY: Columbia University Press, 2018.

Steven Levitsky and Daniel Ziblatt. *Tyranny of the Minority: Why American Democracy Reached the Breaking Point*. New York, NY: Crown, 2023.

Index

G

H

I

J

K

L

M

N

P